Legendary Creatures of the Philippines

Contents

Chapter 1

Agta (mythical creature)

The **agta** is a tall mythical creature, with skin as black as charcoal. These creatures reside in different trees. Among its favorite residences are Santo and Balete trees. They are known to climb down from their perches and roam around the land warning fishermen to stay on land instead of fishing. Then, the agta will push trees down so that the timbers will prevent the fishermen from going to the sea to fish. The agta is just like the kapre, who likes staying in its tree while smoking a rolled cigar. They are usually pictured as naked.[1]

1.1 References

[1] http://awitchinmanila.wordpress.com/occult-manila/mythical-creatures-of-the-philippines

Chapter 2

Alan (legendary creature)

The **Alan** are deformed spirits from the folklore of the Tinguian tribe of the Philippines. They have wings and can fly, and their fingers and toes point backwards.[1]

The *Alan* are said to take drops of menstrual blood, miscarried fetuses, afterbirth, or other reproductive waste and transform them into human children, whom they then raise as their own. They live near springs in extremely fine houses, made of gold and other valuables.

2.1 Basic Legend

A *Tinguian* was once walking along a trail in the woods when he heard a strange sound in a large tree near him, and looking up he was startled to see that it was the home of the Alan-spirits who live in the wood.

He stopped and gazed for a moment at the horrible creatures, large as people, hanging from the limbs of the tree with their heads down like bats. They had wings to fly, and their toes were at the back of their feet, while their long fingers, which pointed backward, were fastened at the wrist.

"Surely," thought the man, "these terrible beings will eat me if they can catch me. I will run away as fast as I can while they are asleep." He tried to run but he was too frightened, and after a few steps he fell face down on the ground.

At this the *Alan* began to wail loudly, for they saw him fall and believed him dead. They came down out of the tree with gold and beads which they laid on him.

After a while the man gathered courage and, jumping up, he cried as loudly as he could, "Go away!"

The *Alan* did not move, but they looked at him and said: "Give us the one bead *nagaba* [a peculiar bead of double effect], and you may have the rest." When the man refused to do this, they were angry and turned away, crying, "Then we are going to burn your house, for you are a bad man."

Thereupon the man went home as fast as he could go, but very soon after that his house burned, for the *Alan* kept their word.

And then...This Alan creature passed his legacy on to those that came forth and were worthy creatures of the gift. So, from generation to generation the Alan creatures can be seen.

2.2 References

[1] Cole, Fay Cooper (2007). *A Study in Tinguian Folk-lore*. Echo Library. p. 14. ISBN 9781406846683.

2.3 Further reading

- Cole, Fay-Cooper (1915). *Traditions of the Tinguian*. Field Museum of Natural History. pp. 14–15. ASIN B0006AH7LY.

- SurLaLune Fairy Tales: Man and the Alan

- SurLaLune Fairy Tales: The Alan and the Hunters

Chapter 3

Amalanhig

Amalanhig (also called 'Maranhig' or 'Amaranhig') are creatures in Visayan mythology, particularly among Hiligaynon speaking groups. *Amalanhig* are *Aswangs* who failed to transfer their monstrosity causing them to rise from their graves to kill humans by biting their necks. Another version that has survived through word-of-mouth recounts that *Amanlanhigs* are said to chase any living person they found and once they reach them, they would tickle the victim until they die, both of laughter and terror. In order to escape from *Amanlanhigs*, one runs in zigzag direction since they can only walk in straight direction due to the stiffness of their body. One would also climb trees or high platforms enough to be out of their reach. One would also run into lakes and rivers since *Amanlanhigs* are scared of deep bodies of water.[1]

The *Amalanhig* are depicted as externally identical to humans, though there is an enlargement of the upper canines in most individuals. The *Amalanhig* is a variant of the vampire native to the Philippines.

3.1 References

[1] "Da Adventure of Pendro Penduko". Archived from the original on 21 September 2008. Retrieved 2008-09-15.

Chapter 4

Amomongo

The **Amomongo** is a creature of Philippine mythology described as hairy, man-sized and ape-like with long nails.[1] The term may have its roots in the Hiligaynon word *amó*, which means "ape" or "monkey". Residents of La Castellana in Negros Occidental refer to the creature as a "wild monkey" that lives in caves near the foot of Mt. Kanlaon. The creature is said to have attacked two residents of the settlement and disemboweled goats and chickens in the area, for the purpose of eating the entrails.[2]

4.1 References

[1] Bayoran, Gilbert (2008-06-13). "Creature terrorizing residents of farms". Visayan Daily Star. Retrieved 2008-06-20.

[2] Delilan, Erwin Ambo (2008-06-16). "Residents on alert vs 'wild monkey'". Sun.Star Bacolod. Retrieved 2008-06-20.

Chapter 5

Anggitay

Anggitay is a creature with an upper body of a female human and of a horse from waist down.[1] They were the Philippine counterpart for the centauride, the female centaurs. They are also believed to be the female counterpart of *Tikbalang*.

Sometimes, they are illustrated to have a single horn in the middle of their forehead just like a unicorn. They were usually said to be attracted to precious gemstones, and jewelries.[1]

5.1 References

[1] "Da Adventure of Pendro Penduko". Archived from the original on 21 September 2008. Retrieved 2008-10-09.

Chapter 6

Aswang

For the 1994 film, see Aswang (1994 film). For the 2011 film, see Aswang (2011 film).

An **Aswang** (or **Asuwang**) is a vampire-like witch ghoul in Filipino folklore and is the subject of a wide variety of myths and stories. Spanish colonists noted that the Aswang was the most feared among the mythical creatures of the Philippines, even in the 16th century.[1]

The myth of the aswang is well known throughout the Philippines, except in the Ilocos region, which is the only region that does not have an equivalent myth.[2] It is especially popular in the Visayan regions such as Capiz, Iloilo, Negros, Bohol, Aklan, Antique, and Siquijor. Other regional names for the aswang include "tik-tik", "wak-wak", "sok-sok", and "kling-kling" .

6.1   Definition

Aswang or "asuwang" is derived from the Sanskrit word Asura which means 'demon'.

Sometimes this creature is called the "bal-bal" or ghoul (*maninilong* in Catanauan, Quezon), which replaces the cadaver with banana trunks after consumption. Aswang stories and definitions vary greatly from region to region and person to person, and no particular set of characteristics can be ascribed to the term. However, the term is mostly used interchangeably with manananggal and are also usually depicted as female.[3]

6.2   Appearance and activities

The wide variety of descriptions in the aswang stories makes it difficult to settle upon a fixed definition of aswang appearances or activities. However, several common themes that differentiate aswangs from other mythological creatures do emerge: Aswangs are shape-shifters. Stories recount aswangs living as regular townspeople. As regular townspeople, they are quiet, shy and elusive. At night, they transform into creatures such as a cat, bat, bird, boar or most often, a dog.

They enjoy eating unborn fetuses and small children, favoring livers and hearts. Some have long proboscises, which they use to suck the children out of their mothers' wombs when they are sleeping in their homes. Some are so thin that they can hide themselves behind a bamboo post. They are fast and silent. Some also make noises, like the Tik-Tik, (the name was derived from the sound it produces) which are louder the farther away the aswang is, to confuse its potential victim; and the Bubuu, an aggressive kind of aswang that makes a sound of a laying hen at midnight. They may also replace their live victims or stolen cadavers with doppelgangers made from tree trunks or other plant materials. This facsimile will return to the victim's home, only to become sick and die. An aswang will also have bloodshot eyes, the result of staying up all night searching for houses where wakes are held to steal the bodies.

Aswangs are physically much more like humans at daytime; they only change their appearance at night when they feel they are in need of food. It has been said that if an aswang married a human, upon their wedding, his or her mate would become an aswang as well but rarely can they reproduce. The couple may hunt together at night but will go in separate directions, either to avoid detection or because they do not like to share their meal.

6.3 Behavior

These creatures are not harmed by sunlight. They are daywalkers. Aswangs can also be befriended, they can talk to you like any normal human being: they laugh, cry, get mad, hurt, and feel envy. These creatures do not harm their neighbors. Neighbors were said to be exempted from their target victims for food, hence the Filipino saying, "Better an aswang than a thief." They search for food in far away places that it would not be too obvious for them. Aswangs are said to be vulnerable during daytime because during that time they do not have the excessive inhuman strength that they have in their nighttime prowl. When people know of their identity, they are hunted down and killed at the barong barong.

6.4 Countermeasures against aswangs

Like vampires, aswangs are repelled or killed by using garlic, salt, and religious artifacts (e.g. Holy water, crucifix, rosary). They are also killed using a whip made entirely of a stingray's tail, which may also be used to repel the creature (aswangs are said to be scared of the sound made by the whip slashing through the air.) it is also said that they cannot step on holy consecrated ground. Decapitation is also a way to destroy an aswang.

Certain agimats and special prayers posted on doors may also repel aswangs. A good example of which is the red and black bead bracelets worn by newborn babies.

It is said that to spot an aswang at daytime, look at their eyes. The person in front of you is an aswang if your reflection is upside-down. Another way of knowing is looking in a *tuwad* manner; that is, bending over and looking at the person from between your legs, upside-down. The person is an aswang if the image of the person is different. It is said that a person without a philtrum is an aswang. A kind of oil made by albularyos is used to detect if an aswang is near the premises. It is said that the oil will boil if an aswang is near.

6.5 References in popular culture

- An Aswang is a Wesen (creature) and the main antagonist in the Season 3, Episode 14 (Mother Dearest) of the NBC TV series "Grimm". The main characters Detectives Nick Burkhardt and Hank Griffin together with police Sergeant Drew Wu fought off an Aswang which tries to suck the fetus out of a pregnant woman who happens to be Wu's childhood friend back in the Philippines in order to extend her lifespan.

- In a 2013 ABS-CBN TV series "Juan dela Cruz", aswangs are the main antagonist which are being hunted by the protagonist Juan who happens to be half-aswang himself.

- A type of Aswang called the "Abuak" is featured in a 2011 Filipino film of the same name. Abuak can transform from human to a raven-like creature that could fly and move underground as it stalks its victim.

- Aswang is featured in a 1994 Filipino film of the same name. It is about a young woman who agreed to be the wife of a rich man who lives in a mansion together with his mother, who happened to be the Aswang.

- An Aswang is depicted as vampirie-like creature in new World of Darkness tabletop RPG game. Description can be found in supplement book called "Antagonists".

- An Aswang character appears in the fourth issue of comedy/horror webcomic Fantastic Crap Comics.

- An Aswang is featured in the sixth episode of the Canadian TV show Lost Girl, and is portrayed as a relatively harmless scavenger Fae.

- Season 11, Episode 3; CSI: "Blood Moon" was aired on October 7, 2010 on CBS Crime Drama TV Series. CSI Quotes: Ray Langston mentioned There's a creature in The Philippines called "Aswang"; a hybrid cross between a vampire & werewolf.

- The Aswang myth is featured in *The Forbidden Room*.

- The Aswang is the subject of the 2011 feature-length documentary *The Aswang Phenomenon*. The film explores the aswang folklore and its effects on Philippine society. The documentary was also the first to uncover the origin of why the Visayan province of Capiz is suspected as the Aswang's home.[4]

6.6 References

[1] Scott, William Henry (1994). *Barangay: Sixteenth Century Philippine Culture and Society*. Quezon City: Ateneo de Manila University Press. ISBN 971-550-135-4.

[2] Tan, Michael (2008-10-26). "Aswang! Aswang!". *Sunday Inquirer Magazine*.

[3] File:Carljames|thumbnail

[4] Clark, Jordan (2011) *The Aswang Phenomenon* Documentary, High Banks Entertainment Ltd. https://www.youtube.com/watch?v=2ePhqoyLpXQ

6.7 Further reading

- Cruz, Neal (2008-10-31). "As I See It: Philippine mythological monsters". *Philippine Daily Inquirer*.

- Eugenio, Damiana (2002). *Philippine Folk Literature: The Legends*. Matt Asombrado Paculba City: University of the Philippines Press. p. 490. ISBN 971-542-357-4.

- Ramos, Maximo D. (1971). *Creatures of Philippine Lower Mythology*. Quezon City: University of the Philippines Press. ISBN 971-06-0691-3.

- Ocampo, Ambeth (2010-02-16). "Looking Back: 'Aswang' and counter-insurgency". *Philippine Daily Inquirer*.

Chapter 7

Bakunawa

The **Bakunawa**, also spelled **Bakonawa**, **Baconaua**, or **Bakonaua**, is a dragon in Philippine mythology that is often represented as a gigantic sea serpent. It is believed to be the cause of eclipses.

It appears as a giant sea serpent with a mouth the size of a lake, a red tongue, whiskers, gills, small wires at its sides, and two sets of wings, one is large and ash-gray while the other is small and is found further down its body.

7.1 Mythology

Tales about the *Tabashie* say that it is the cause of eclipses. During ancient times, Filipinos believe that there are seven moons created by *Bathala* to light up the sky. The *Tabashie*, amazed by their beauty, would rise from the ocean and swallow the moons whole, angering Bathala and causing them to be mortal enemies.

To keep the moons from completely being swallowed by the *Tabashie*, ancient Filipinos would go out of their homes with pans and pots, and would make noise in order to scare the Tabashie into spitting out the moon back into the sky. Some of the people in the villages would play soothing sounds with their musical instruments, in hopes that the dragon would fall into a deep sleep. Thus, the brave men of the village hoped that while the dragon was hypnotized by the musical sounds they could somehow slay the dragon. Although the dragon was known as a "moon eater" it was also known as a "man eater".

Other tales tell that the *Tabashie* has a sister in the form of a sea turtle. The sea turtle would visit a certain island in the Philippines in order to lay its eggs. However, locals soon discovered that every time the sea turtle went to shore, the water seemed to follow her, thus reducing the island's size. Worried that their island would eventually disappear, the locals killed the sea turtle.

When the *Tabashie* found out about this, it arose from the sea and ate the moon. The people were afraid so they prayed to *Bathala* to punish the creature. Bathala refused but instead told them to bang some pots and pans in order to disturb the serpent. The moon is then regurgitated while the Tabashie disappeared, never to be seen again.

The island where the sea turtle lays its eggs is said to exist today. Some sources say that the island might just be one of the Turtle Islands.

Others tell how the *Tabashie* fell in love with a human girl in one of the native tribes. The head of the tribe found out about their affair and had their house burned to ashes. The *Tabashie*, finding out about this, became immersed in anger and tried to take revenge by eating all the 7 moons. When the *Tabashie* was about to eat the last one, *Bathala* took action and punished the *Tabashie* by banishing it from its home away from the sea. It also tells that the reason of the eclipses is how the *Tabashie* is trying to come back to its home and deceased family.

Some ((Himalayo)(Filipino)) elders Tabashieis a moving Isle with communities mounted at the back, it is said to believe that has 2 classification the flying Tabashie and the land Tabashie.

7.2 Literature

There is a short *Hiligaynon* song in 3/4 time that children used to sing during lunar eclipses:

7.3 Similar creatures

Other serpentine/dragon deities are also found in other myths in the Philippines. These include the *Bawa*, the *Bauta*, *Mameleu* or *Mamelen* or *Nanreben*, and *Marcupo* or *Macupo* of *Hiligaynon* mythology, *Buwaya* or *Nono* of *Tagalog* mythology, and *Mikonawa* or *Mikunawa* or *Minokawa* of *Bagobo* mythology.

7.4 Sword hilt ornaments

Figures of the *Bakunawa's* head decorate the hilts of many ancient Filipino swords. These swords that originate in Panay are said to bestow upon the *hangaway* or *mandirigma* (sacred warriors) the fearful presence and power of the *Bakunawa* (or whatever deity/animal they have on their deity hilt) when they wield their swords in combat.

7.5 Games

A children's game called Bulan Bulan, Buwan Buwan, or Bakunawa is played in the Philippines. It has 6-8 players arranged in a circle.

A player acts as the buwan/bulan (moon) while another player act as the *Bakunawa* (eclipse), chosen either through Jack-en-poy, *"maalis taya"*, or *"maiba taya."* The other participants stand in a circle facing the center and holding each other's hands. The buwan/bulan stands inside the circle while the *Bakunawa* stands outside.

7.5.1 Objective

The object of the game is for the *Bakunawa* to tag or touch the *buwan/bulan*. The rest of the players try to prevent the bakunawa from doing so by holding on to each other and running around the circle as fast as they can while not letting go of the ones next to them.

For the *Bakunawa* to get into the circle, he or she asks one of the players, "What chain is this?" and when the player replies, "This is an iron chain," the *Bakunawa* should ask another player because an iron chain is supposed to be unbreakable. A player who wants to let the bakunawa in can say, "This is an abaca chain," and should let go of his or her hold. This is usually done when the player playing as the bakunawa is tired from running around.

The *malatikantumanlak* can also try to get in by going under the linked hands. If the player chosen as the bakunawa is fast and small enough, this can be done easily. As soon as the bakunawa succeeds in getting in, the players forming the circle should let the buwan out of the circle.

The *Bakunawa* then tries to break out of the linked hands to try to get out to catch the buwan/bulan. When the *Bakunawa* succeeds in catching the buwan/bulan, they exchange places, or if both of them are too tired, another pair from the circle of players is chosen as the new *Bakunawa* and *buwan/bulan*.

7.6 See also

- Coi Coi-Vilu

7.7 References

Chapter 8

Bal-Bal

For Central Asian funeral monuments ("balbal"), see Kurgan stelae.

In Philippine mythology, a **Bal-Bal** is a monster that steals corpses whether it is in a funeral or grave and feeds on them. It has a strong sense of smell for dead human bodies. It also has claws and teeth sharp enough to rip the clothing of the dead. Since it eats nothing but corpses, it has a foul breath. Once this monster has spotted and eaten the corpse, it will leave the trunk of a banana tree in the coffin creating an illusion of the stolen body to trick people.[1]

Bal-Bal was also associated to *Aswang*, *Amalanhig*, and even to *Busaw*, which were all flesh eaters. They were classified to one of the most fearful creatures in the Philippines because of their appearance. They were even described and compared to the vampire of the western continents.[2] I

8.1 References

[1] "Da Adventure of Pendro Penduko". Archived from the original on 21 September 2008. Retrieved 2008-09-15.

[2] "Amalanhig". Archived from the original on 19 September 2008. Retrieved 2008-09-15.

Template:Philippine bulbol

Chapter 9

Balete Drive

Balete Drive is a two-lane undivided street and main thoroughfare in the New Manila District, in Quezon City, in Metro Manila, Philippines. The road is an undivided carriageway, that is, a road without median. The road is a major route of jeepneys and cabs, serving the New Manila area, connecting Eulogio Rodriguez Sr. Boulevard and Nicanor Domingo Streets in Quezon City.

The road is famous for the antique and century old Spanish houses and Balete Trees that line the road. The road is also notable for the haunting legends that it had.

9.1 Route description

Balete Drive connects the long span between Eulogio Rodriguez Sr. Boulevard and Nicanor Domingo Street in New Manila, Quezon City. The Balete Drive corner at E. Rodriguez is a bustling business area mushroomed with fast foods and other establishments.

This north end of the Balete Drive starts at a dead end next to the Diliman Creek, 160 metres (520 ft) north of Eulogio Rodriguez, Sr. Boulevard[1] Running in the NNE to SSE direction, it ends in a T-junction with the Nicanor Domingo Street near the San Juan Reservoir for a total length of 1.3 kilometres (0.81 mi).[2] One of its major intersection is with the Aurora Boulevard, a major road which leads to Cubao, a major commercial district in Quezon City. The LRT-2 Betty Go-Belmonte station is located 330 metres (1,080 ft) east of this junction.[3]

9.2 History

Balete Drive was named after a gargantuan balete tree that used to stand in the middle of the road. The road, although the exact construction date is unknown, had been cemented and asphalted and became a main thoroughfare during the regime of President Ferdinand Marcos in the early 1970s.[4] There are several Spanish houses in the area, including the famous 200-year-old "Centennial House", which supports the claim that Balete Drive has been in use since the late Spanish era towards the end of the 19th century.[5]

9.3 Haunting legend

The street is reported to be haunted with tales circulating since the 1950s.[4][5] Many reports that the old Spanish homes in the area were haunted, or being guarded by their former, dead Spanish owners. The most famous case and the case most reported is the story of a "White Lady" frequently being seen in that site, according to a famous Philippine urban legend. Also, other mythical creatures from the Philippine folklore were also sometimes seen around the site, like elves and fairies. A Sighting of a Kapre, a large, smoking black giant, was reported from that area once.

The Balete Drive

9.3.1 Reports

Most of the reports describes a White Veiled Lady, a popular entity in the Philippine folklore. The White Lady is frequently seen in the portion of the road from the intersection of the road with the Mabolo Street up to the Intersection of the road with the Bougainvilla Street. The reports commonly came from taxi drivers, particularly those driving on the graveyard shift between 12:00 am and 3:00 am. The reports described commonly fits the descriptions on the reports involving the infamous Teresa Fidalgo reports from Portugal, on account of the white lady, either calling over to ride on their cab or suddenly appearing inside the car.[6][7] By Junox the Great. and Jereme Grapa

9.3.2 Unconventional explanations

Some of the unconventional theories attempting to explain the tales about the neighborhood are very similar to the Teresa Fidalgo stories. The "white lady" is said to be the ghost a teenage girl that died in a car accident in the area many years ago. Another variation of the tale is that the girl was raped by a cab driver. The above reason is used to explain why the lady always shows herself to cab and taxi drivers.[6][8][9]

From the Philippine folklore, Balete trees are always considered magical, and sometimes, kingdoms of spirits, which is another unconventional explanation for the eerie and mysterious tales that occur in the vicinity.

9.3.3 Skeptical explanations

The skeptical and conventional explanations, of course, dismiss the entire story and all tales and reports as hoaxes. The tale is believed to be a hoax of a newspaper reporter.[9] It is also presumed that it is made by a group of college students on surveillance on how fast a rumor can spread.[6]

The most accepted explanation, however, is the possibility of a mirage or an illusion. The floating lady is dismissed as an optical illusion caused by the car's headlights.[6] The same explanation is given to another alleged haunted street in Quezon City, the Calle Tres Marias in Barangay bahay toro in Project 6, which is said to be the habitat of strange cat-like creatures.[7]

9.4 Zoning laws

The segment of the Balete Drive from Aurora Boulevard to Eulogio Rodriguez, Sr. Ave has been zoned by the Bureau of Internal Revenue for regular residential and commercial purposes.[10]

9.5 In popular culture

The movie *Hiwaga sa Balete Drive* (Mystery on Balete Drive) is a Filipino movie based on the ghost that allegedly roam the road. It was filmed in 1988 with the white lady portrayed by Filipina singer-actress Zsa Zsa Padilla. In the story, she died during the Spanish Colonial Era, but her spirit is forever roaming, searching for her undying love. Some of the actual scenes were filmed on Balete Drive. The movie is frequently shown during Halloween on Philippine television. [11]

9.6 See also

- Major roads in Metro Manila

- Aurora Boulevard

- Haunted highway

9.7 References

[1] "Kamuning Road". Google Maps. Retrieved on April 18, 2012.

[2] "Balete Drive". Google Maps. Retrieved on April 18, 2012.

[3] "Balete Drive". Google Maps. Retrieved on April 18, 2012.

[4] Ellalynn De Vera and Charissa M. Lucci (July 17, 2005). "The Haunting of Balete drive". *The Manila Bulletin*. Retrieved August 25, 2012.

[5] Philippines Insider. "Myths Surrounding Balete Drive". Philippines Insider. Retrieved August 26, 2012.

[6] Yap, Dj (Nov 1, 2005). "Balete may be official "haunted" site". Philippine Daily Inquirer. Retrieved 18 April 2012. Check date values in: |year= / |date= mismatch (help)

[7] Magbanua, Lyndon John. "The Story of the White Lady of Balete drive". *September 12, 2011*. The Mystified.com. Retrieved August 26, 2012.

[8] Priscelina Patajo-Legasto (2008). *Philippine Studies: Have We Gone Beyond St. Louis?*. UP Press. pp. 349–. ISBN 978-971-542-591-9. Retrieved 18 April 2012.

[9] Dianne De Las Casas; Zarah C. Gagatiga (30 September 2011). *Tales from the 7,000 Isles: Filipino Folk Stories*. ABC-CLIO. pp. 119–. ISBN 978-1-59884-698-0. Retrieved 18 April 2012.

[10] "Zonal Values – RDO No. 39-South Quezon City – Barangay Mariana". Bureau of Internal Revenue (Philippines). Retrieved on April 18, 2012.

[11] *Hiwaga sa Balete Drive* at the Internet Movie Database. Retrieved on April 18, 2012.

Chapter 10

Batibat

The **Batibat** or **Bangungot** is a vengeful demon found in Ilocano folklore. These demons were blamed as the cause of the fatal nocturnal disease called bangungot. A batibat takes the form of a huge, old, fat woman that resides in trees. They usually come in contact with humans when the tree that they reside in is felled and made into a support post for a house. This causes them to migrate into holes found in the post. The batibat forbids humans from sleeping near its post. When a person does sleep near it, the batibat transforms to its true form and attacks that person. It sits upon the chest of its victim until he suffocates. To ward off the batibat, one should bite one's thumb or wiggle one's toes. In this way, the person will awaken from the nightmare induced by the batibat.[1]

10.1 See also

- Brugada syndrome
- Sleep apnea
- Sleep paralysis
- Pesanta
- Lietuvēns

10.2 References

[1] Ramos, Maximo D. (1971). *Creatures of Philippine Lower Mythology.* Philippines: University of the Philippines Press.

Chapter 11

Berbalang (legendary creature)

The **Berbalang** are creatures of Filipino myth. Having a human appearance, they resemble vampires but with wings and slanted eyes. They dig up graves in order to eat corpses.

The following account of an encounter with the Berbalangs occurs in Rupert T. Gould's book *Oddities*, published in 1928:[1]

In the 1896 Journal of the Asiatic Society of Bengal, Mr. Ethelbert Forbes Skertchley of Hong Kong reported the remarkable story of the Berbalangs of Cagayan Sulu:[1]

"In the center of the island is a small village, the inhabitants of which owe allegiance to neither of the two chiefs. These people are called 'Berbalangs', and the Cagayans live in great fear of them. These Berbalangs are ghouls, and must eat human flesh occasionally or they would die. You can always tell them, because the pupils of their eyes are not round, but just narrow slits like those of a cat. They dig open the graves and eat the entrails of the corpses; but in Cagayan the supply is limited, so when they feel the craving for a feed of human flesh they go away into the grass, and, having carefully hidden their bodies, hold their breath and fall into a trance. Their astral bodies are then liberated.... They fly away, and entering a house make their way into the body of one of the occupants and feed on their entrails..... The Berbalangs may be heard coming, as they make a moaning noise which is loud at a distance and dies away to a feeble moan as they approach. When they are near you the sound of their wings may be heard and the flashing lights of their eyes can be seen like dancing fire-flies in the dark. Should you be the happy possessor of a Coconut pearl you are safe, but otherwise the only way to beat them off is to cut at them with a kris, the blade of which has been rubbed with the juice of a lime. If you see the lights and hear the moaning in front of you, wheel suddenly round and make a cut in the opposite direction. Berbalangs always go by contraries and are never where they appear to be."[1]

"The cocoa-nut pearl, a stone like an opal sometimes found in the cocoa-nut, is the only really efficacious charm against their attacks; and it is only of value to the finder, as its magic powers cease when it is given away. When the finder dies the pearl loses its luster and becomes dead. The juice of limes sprinkled on a grave will prevent the Berbalangs from entering it, so all the dead are buried either under or near the houses, and the graves are sprinkled daily with fresh lime juice."[1]

11.1 References

[1] Gould, Rupert T., "Berbalangs," *Oddities*, 1928.

Chapter 12

Berberoka

The people from *Apayao*, *Abra* and *Ilocos Norte* believe and fear a swamp creature called **Berberoka**. It lures victims by sucking water in the pond enough for a number fish to come into surface. When the potential victims get attracted to the school of fish, the Berberoka drowns them by hosing water and swallowing them afterwards.[1]

They were compared to the Greek naiads, the nymphs of water elements. They have the ability to suck all the water in a swamp or lake. Also, many old folks believed that they use water to attack their enemies. They discharge a large amount of water (just like a fire extinguisher) to their victims until they drown.[2]

12.1 References

[1] "Da Adventure of Pendro Penduko". Retrieved 2008-09-15.

[2] *Mga Engkanto: A Bestiary of Filipino Fairies*. Philippines: eLf ideas Publication. 2003.

Chapter 13

Bungisngis

Bungisngis is a giant cyclops in Philippine folklore. This giant, purported to dwell in Meluz, Orion, Bataan, is described as is always laughing.[1] The literal meaning of the name *Bungingis* is derived from the Tagalog word *ngisi* which means "to giggle".[2]

Having a humanoid shape, it has large teeth which are always showing, and its upper lip covers its face when it is thrown back. Two long tusks project from the side of its mouth. The cyclops only eye, is found in the middle of its forehead,[1] but this is compensated by its strong sense of hearing. It has also displays unusual strength. In the Filipino tale "The Three Friends - The Monkey, The Dog and The Carabao, The giant is able to lift the carabao and throw it with such force that it ends knee-deep in the ground.[3] However, despite its strength, the bungisngis is easily outwitted and quickly panics.[4][5] In the tale of the Three Friends, Monkey's tricks led him to his death.[3]

13.1 References

[1] Ramos, Maximo D. (1990) [1971]. *Creatures of Philippine Lower Mythology*. Quezon: Phoenix Publishing. p. 76. ISBN 971-06-0691-3.

[2] Viloria, Manuel (November 13, 2005). "Philippine Lower Mythology". viloria.com. Retrieved October 9, 2008.

[3] Fansler, Dean Spouill (2009). *Filipino Popular Tales*. BiblioBazaar, LLC. p. 31. ISBN 978-0-559-95004-9. Retrieved May 9, 2009.

[4] Paraiso, Salvador; Jose Juan Paraiso (2003). *The Balete Book: A Collection of Demons, Monsters, Elves and Dwarfs from the Philippine Lower Mythology*. Giraffee Books. p. 57. ISBN 971-8832-79-3.

[5] "Magical Creatures and Non Human beings of the Philippines". Filipino Forum.Net. Archived from the original on May 1, 2008. Retrieved October 9, 2008.

Chapter 14

Busaw

Busaw is a legendary creature that resembles humans in appearance and behavior, raising farm animals and planting root crops. However, its favorite food is humans, resulting in scattered human skeletons on the grounds of its dwelling place.[1]

The *Busaw* was a ghoul and corpse thief. An evil spirit who looked and behaved like ordinary human beings by day, it listened for sounds of death in the evenings, and dwelled in large trees near cemeteries. It had pointed teeth, hooked nails and a long tongue. It took banana tree trunks to replace the dead as it stole the corpses out of their coffins. Then, spiriting the corpse off after first turning it into a pig, the *Busaw* would feast on it and even try to feed it to their human neighbors during the day in order to turn them into ghouls like itself. To ward the *Busaw* off, all corpses should be washed completely with vinegar and strong-smelling herbs. Salt is also a *Busaw* repellent.[2]

14.1 References

[1] "Da Adventure of Pendro Penduko". Retrieved 2008-09-15.

[2] "Filipino Ghosts and Spirits". Retrieved 2008-09-15.

Chapter 15

Dalaketnon

Dalaketnon are the bad *engkanto*. *Dalaketnons* appeared as tall and handsome males and beautiful females. They dress in fashionable manner, live in mansions and try to fit in with mortal people. Some believe that the only way to *Dalaket*, their dwelling place, is by entering the *Dalaket* trees. These creatures abduct people and take them to their world. They hold a feast for their victims and force them to eat the Black Rice that put them under their spell making them their slaves.[1]

Dalaketnons were known to be rather beautiful elitists. They have a bit of a *coño*, a kind of telekinesis as well as corporeal duplication—meaning they could generate tangible, living copies of themselves indefinitely, and their hairs and eyes turn white whenever they power manifests.[1]

The *Dalaketnons* have a normal contact with humans but the humans do not know that they are engkanto. Old folks believed that *Dalaketnons* can change an ordinary human into creatures like them. They use a magical black rice to change their victims into a *Dalaketnon*. It was also believed that they were the mortal enemies of the good *engkanto*. They are from the royal blood of bad engkantos that served as their ruler. They were associated to be the masters of *Aswang*, *Bal-Bal*, *Wak Wak*, *Manananggal*, *Amalanhig*, and even *Tiktik*.[2]

15.1 References

[1] "Da Adventure of Pendro Penduko". Retrieved 2008-09-15.

[2] *Mga Engkanto: A Bestiary of Filipino Fairies*. Philippines: eLf ideas Publication. 2003.

Chapter 16

Diwata

For the Abra song, see Diwata (song).
For satellite, see Diwata (satellite).
"Lambana" redirects here. For the genus of moth, see Lambana (moth).

In Philippine mythology, a **diwata**, based on Sanskrit *devata* (देवता) and also known as **encantada** from Spanish, is a dryad-like spirit which is benevolent or neutral and invoked ritually for positive crop growth, health, and fortune; they may also incur illness or misfortune if not given proper respect.[1] They are said to reside in large trees, such as acacia and balete and are the guardian spirits of nature, casting blessings or curses upon those who bring benefits or harm to the forests and mountains. They have their origin in the Devata beings included in Hinduism and Buddhism. The Laguna Copperplate dated 900 AD also makes mention of a Chief of Medang in Java, Indonesia referred as representative of the Chief of Diwata in Butuan, Mindanao island.

The term "diwata" has taken on various levels of meaning since its concept's assimilation into the mythology of the pre-colonial Filipinos. It is sometimes loosely used to refer to a generic type of beings much like "elf" or "fairy," or very specific ones as mentioned above. It has been noted that the term "diwata" is synonymous to "anito," and that the usage of the word "diwata" is more prevalent in the Southern Philippines, while "anito" takes its place in the Northern areas.

16.1   Characteristics

Although there are numerous and varied accounts as to what they should look like, a general trend may be observed in that they are normally human in appearance—beautiful and seemingly ageless at that—save for some distinct characteristics. This may take the form of not having a philtrum or having continuously smooth and supple skin that somehow resemble fingernails, without any wrinkled parts as in the elbows and knees. They also tend to be fairer than average, as pale skin has been associated with the supernatural even during pre-colonial times (for example, the "white lady" belief is prevalent in the East and Southeast Asian regions).

16.2   Types

A *male diwata* is also called *enkanto*, and it resides primarily in the sea. It is customary for Filipino fishermen to offer meat and other delicacies to the *enkanto* by throwing them into the sea, after a day's bountiful catch. Popular mythology states that the diwata who live in large trees do not live in them like you would imagine a monkey. It is believed they actually live inside the trunk of the tree itself, in the form of a spirit. In the Philippines, it is common to see tree trunks of trees with trunks larger than 5' or 6" in diameter left standing when trees have been cut. This is believed to prevent the spirit from being released, as it is not known if he is a "white" or "black" spirit. If he is a black spirit, it is believed he can cause serious misfortune to the one who stole his home.

16.3 Popular culture

16.3.1 Comics

In the comics character created by Gener Pedrina for the Sanduguan Universe, Diwata is a half-human and half-encantada whose real name is Maria Klarissa Valiente.

16.3.2 Television

In the television sitcom *Okay ka, Fairy Ko* created by MZET productions, diwatas live in a mythical world named Enkantasya where Ina Magenta is the Queen of the diwatas. Ina Magenta's daughter, Faye, is married to Enteng Kabisote, a human.

Diwata have also been featured on GMA Network fantasy series *Encantadia* and *Mulawin* whereby diwatas are a race of supernatural being living in Encantadia, a dimension beyond the human world.[2] However, the depiction of a diwata on both series have European influences as pure diwatas were shown to have pointed ears like elves, one of them is Cassiopeia and some resemble fairies, like Muyak, human-like diwatas are born from a diwata and another encantado. All diwatas and encantados reside in the *Kingdom of Lireo*. A diwata or an encantado that has royal blood is called *Sang'gre*, which can be distinguished by their markings on their back, the *nga* character from the Baybayin script. The Queen of the diwata in Lireo carries the title of *Ynang Reyna*. Lirean society is matriarchal and only a *Sang'gre* in the matriarch line may ascend the throne.

Another television series from GMA Network, Amaya, depicts diwata as goddesses who may be called upon through a ritual. The series revolves around the life of Amaya, a binukot (kept maiden) and her fate to become the most powerful woman of her time. It is set during the pre-colonial times of the Philippines. The diwata shown were:

- Maguayen, who ferries the souls of the dead to Sulad (Purgatory).

- Pandaki, who can change a fate of a dungan (soul)She also brings good dungan from Sulad to Saad(Heaven) to be an umalagad.

- Malandok, goddess of war.

- Bakunawa (A Dragon), guardian of Sulad.

In another GMA Network TV series, Indio, diwata are gods or goddesses that can be called or prayed upon. Indio is about a man with a diwata mother and a human father who grew up after the pre-colonial times and during the Spanish colonial period, he protects the Filipinos from the Spaniards. Many diwata are shown in Indio:

- Makaptan, the supreme god.

- Ynaguiginid, war and earth goddess(successor of Maladok) .

- Magayon, goddess of flying animals, wood goddess.

- Lalahon, goddess fire and volcanoes.

- Lidagat, water goddess.

- Libulan, moon goddess.

- Lihangin, wind goddess.

- Dalikmata, goddess of eye diseases, ice goddess.

- Adlaw, sun god.

- Barangaw, rainbow god.

- Ribung Linti, lightning god.

- Lisantonillo, god of blessngs.

- Burigadang Pada Sinaklang Bulawan, goddess of greed.

- Paiburong, god of the middle world. He is the brother of Burigadang Pada.

- Makabosog, god of gluttony.

- Sidapa, god of death.

- Pandaki, goddess who saves souls for a better fate.

- Magwayen, goddess who ferries the souls to the land of the dead.

- Alunsina, goddess of eastetn skies

The term, *lambana*, an old Tagalog word for a drawing symbol or picture that represents a deity of the ancient pagan religion of the Tagalog people was recently used in fantasy-themed television shows such as ABS-CBN's *Pedro Penduko* as a term for "small fairies". Although, it can also be argued that the term was first used in Encantadia as a reference to Muyak, and later on in Luna Mystika where it was used to identify the characters played by Pauleen Luna and Michelle Madrigal.

16.3.3   Music

Diwata is a Filipino singer-comedienne who made a mark with the Tagalog remake of the English song "Sincerely" and became well known with "Sisirin Mo," a naughty song with double meaning that titillated the masses' imagination from her self-titled album "Diwata". This album launched a whole new genre of songs that shocked the sensibilities of the predominantly Catholic Philippines in the year 2001. In 2014, rapper Abra released a song titled "Diwata", which features Parokya Ni Edgar vocalist Chito Miranda, from his self-titled debut album.

16.3.4   Literature

Diwata is the primary character in the play *Speech and Debate* written in 2007 by Stephen Karam. The character constitutes an ironic representation of the Diwata, as an awkward, socially rejected high school student intent on creating her own club to catalyze the downfall of her closed-minded drama teacher.

16.3.5   Cinema

The independent film 'Faraway' focuses on a woman and her quest to find the Diwata tribe. [3]

16.4   See also

- Devata, deities, divine beings or lesser gods in Hinduism and Buddhism concept

- Hyang, similar concept in ancient Indonesia

- Kami, similar concept in Japanese Shinto faith

16.5 References

[1] William Henry Scott's *Barangay: Sixteenth-Century Philippine Culture and Society*, 1994 ISBN 9789715501354

[2] "'I Juander': Naniniwala pa ba sa diwata si Juan?". GMA News. July 15, 2013.

[3] http://www.imdb.com/title/tt2447338/

Chapter 17

Ekek

In Philippine mythology, **Ekek** (or **Ek Ek**) are creatures who are bird-like humans. They are winged-humans who search for victims at night. They hunger for flesh and blood. They are usually described s as flying creatures that look like the *Manananggal* but are unable to divide or split their body. Apart from the *Manananggal*, they are also associated to the *Wak Wak* because of some similar characteristics. The only difference between a *Wak Wak* and *Ekek* is that *Ekek* has a bill like birds whereas the *Wak Wak* has none.[1]

The *Ekek* can transform into a huge bird/bat at night and prowls. Similar to the Manananggal, the *Ekek* looks for sleeping pregnant women. Then it extends a very long proboscis into the womb and kills the fetus by draining its blood. It is said that while this is taking place, a "ek-ek-ek" sound is often heard. The *Ekek* fools people into thinking it is far by producing a faint sound when it is actually near.

17.1 References

[1] *Mga Engkanto: A Bestiary of Filipino Fairies*. Philippines: eLf ideas Publication. 2003.

Chapter 18

Engkanto

Engkanto are environmental spirits that have the ability to appear in human form.[1] They are often associated with the spirits of ancestors in the Philippines.[2][3][4] They are also characterized as forest spirits or elves.[5] Belief in their existence has likely existed for centuries,[4] and continues to this day.[6]

18.1 Appearance

Engkanto have many similarities to humans in that they age, appear to have male and female sexes, can suffer from illness and indeed even die. They are an object mythology for many Filipinos they normally appear to be beautiful having blue eyes, fair complexion and golden hair.[4] They may however have unusual features such as high-bridged noses, fair skin, blond hair and lack of philtrum. They are also known to be taller than human beings.[5] Other variants exhibit sexual dimorphism such as Bagobo spirits which are separated into the female *tahamaling* and the male *mahomanay*. The female spirit is alleged to have red complexion while the male have a fair complexion.[5] Their dwellings will normally appear as natural features, for example large rocks or trees, although to humans they have befriended they can appear as magnificent palaces.[4] These creatures prefer large trees such as the *balete* in which they also place their belongings.[5]

18.2 Capabilities

Engkanto are most commonly known for their malignant effects, those the Engkanto favour have become depressed, suffered from madness or even disappeared for days or months, possibly as a result of the human being possessed.[4][7] They are also said to be capable of causing fevers and skin diseases such as boils. These spirits also sometimes lead travelers astray in the forest or even kidnap them this however is said be avoided by bringing an "*Anting-anting*" or "*Agimat*" a piece of a magical charm or amulet that keeps away evil spirits & prevents them from doing any harm.[3] However if they do favour someone they are generous and capable of bringing power and riches to that person. Shaman often try to commune with Engkanto on holy days to obtain better healing powers from them as well as learning how to better deal with evil spirits.[4]

18.3 Study

Francisco Demetrio made a study of 87 folk stories from Visayas and Mindanao relating to Engkanto. He contended the Engkanto were based on early European friars.[2][4]

18.4 References

[1] Silliman University, James W. Chapman Research Foundation (1977). "Silliman Journal". *Silliman Journal* (Silliman University): 354. Retrieved 2008-06-21.

[2] Aguilar, Filomeno V. (1998). *Clash of Spirits*. University of Hawaii Press. ISBN 0-8248-2082-7.

[3] Gailyn Van Rheenen, Gailyn Van Rheenan (2006). *Contextualization And Syncretism: Navigating Cultural Currents*. William Carey Library. ISBN 0-87808-387-1. Retrieved 2008-06-21.

[4] • Demetrio, Francisco (1969). "The Engkanto Belief: An Essay in Interpretation". *Asian Folklore Studies* **28** (1): 77–90. doi:10.2307/1177781. JSTOR 1177781.

[5] Ramos, Maximo D. (1971). *Creatures of Philippine Lower Mythology*. Philippines: University of the Philippines Press. pp. 55–56. OCLC 804797. ISBN 971-06-0691-3 (Quezon City Press, 1990)

[6] • Borchgrevink, Axel (2003). "Ideas of Power in the Philippines". *Cultural Dynamics* **15** (1): 41–69. doi:10.1177/0921374003015001 Retrieved 2008-06-19.

[7] Tremlett, Paul-François (2007). "The Ethics of Suspicion in the Study of Religions". *DISKUS* **8**. Retrieved 2008-06-20.

Chapter 19

Kapre

Kapre is a Philippine mythical creature that could be characterized as a tree demon. It is described as being a tall (7 to 9 ft), dark, muscular creature. Kapres are normally described as having a strong smell that would attract human attention. The term kapre comes from the Arabic "kafir", meaning a non-believer in Islam. The early Arabs and the Moors used it to refer to the non-Muslim Dravidians who were dark-skinned and went to war against. The term was later brought to the Philippines by the Spanish who had previous contact with the Moors. Some historians speculate that the legend was propagated by the Spanish to prevent Filipinos from assisting any escaped African slaves they sometimes imported from Latin-America. The Kapre itself holds a large Cigar, an item which originated from the ancient Mayans of Latin-America.[1] The similar dark skin color of escaped African slaves from Latin America to Dravidians from South India have caused the former to be equated with the latter.

19.1   Natural habitat and attire

Kapres are said to dwell in big trees like acacias, mangoes, bamboo and banyan (known in the Philippines as *balete*). It is also mostly seen sitting under those trees. The Kapre is said to wear the indigenous Northern Philippine loincloth known as *bahag*, and according to some, often wears a belt which gives the kapre the ability to be invisible to humans. In some versions, the kapre is supposed to hold a magical white stone, a little smaller in size than a quail egg. Should any person happen to obtain this stone, the kapre could grant wishes.

19.2   Behavior

Kapres are not necessarily considered to be evil, unlike the Aswang. Kapres may make contact with people to offer friendship, or if it is attracted to a woman. If a Kapre befriends any human, especially because of love, the Kapre will consistently follow its "love interest" throughout life. Also, if one is a friend of the Kapre then that person will have the ability to see it and if they were to sit on it then any other person would be able to see the huge entity.

Kapres are also said to play pranks on people, frequently making travelers become disoriented and lose their way in the mountains or in the woods. They are also believed to have the ability to confuse people even in their own familiar surroundings; for instance, someone who forgets that they are in their own garden or home is said to have been tricked by a Kapre. Reports of experiencing Kapre enchantment include that of witnessing rustling tree branches, even if the wind is not strong. Some more examples would be hearing loud laughter coming from an unseen being, witnessing lots of smoke from the top of a tree, seeing big fiery eyes during night time from a tree, as well as actually seeing a Kapre walking in forested areas. It is also believed that abundant fireflies in woody areas are the embers from the Kapre's lit Cigars or Tobacco pipe.

19.3 See also

- Aswang

- Manananggal

- Ghosts in Filipino culture

- Tikbalang

- Nephilim

- Troll

19.4 Further reading

- Cruz, Neal (2008-10-31), "As I See It: Philippine mythological monsters", *Philippine Daily Inquirer*

19.5 References

[1] Mayan word "Sikar" may have inspired the modern word "Cigar"

19.6 External links

- Filipino Folklore: Kapre

Chapter 20

Kataw (Philippine mythology)

The **Kataw** is one of the merfolk in the Philippine Mythology. In Visayan, *Kataw* was believed to have higher rankings than other water and sea creatures as those of *Sirena*, *Sireno* and *Siyokoy*. It is believed that the *Kataws* are the reigning rulers of the kingdom *Bantay Tubig*.[1]

Based on physical features, *Kataws*, along the *Sirena* and *Sireno*, were the *Bantay Tubig*-creatures that bear likeness to human while *Siyokoy* are those that resemble water-creatures. Unlike *Sirena*, they have feet instead of tails but they have gills on their bodies and fins in their arms. These marine creatures disguises into fishermen asking for help. When approached by mortals, the *Kataws* drown them into the abyss.[2]

According to old folks, *Kataws* have the ability to manipulate and control water-type elements and related forces such as pressure, tides, waves, bubbles and the likes. Also, they can change water to ice .[3]

20.1 References

[1] *Mga Engkanto: A Bestiary of Filipino Fairies*. Philippines: eLf ideas Publication. 2003.

[2] "Da Adventure of Pendro Penduko". Retrieved 2008-10-09.

[3] *Mga Engkanto: A Bestiary of Filipino Fairies*. Philippines: eLf ideas Publication. 2003.

Chapter 21

Kumakatok

The **Kumakatok** (*door knockers*) are a group of three robed figures believed by many in the Philippines to knock on doors in the middle of the night, bringing bad omens. They allegedly look like humans but wear hoods which obscure their faces to some extent. One resembles a young female while the other two look like old people.

A visit from the Kumakatok is usually an omen of death, as either the eldest or an ill member of the house visited will subsequently die. The visits are supposedly more frequent after a disease outbreak. Residences of Luzon and Visayas at one time painted white crosses on their doors to ward off the Kumakatok. This trend was said to cause the trio to switch from residences to government buildings, hospitals, and even churches.

Reported sightings of the Kumakatok have decreased significantly since World War II. One explanation is that many buildings were destroyed at that time, leaving the Kumatakok few doors to knock upon.

21.1 External Links

- Flipino Folklore: Kumakatik

21.2 References

- Paraiso, Salvador; Jose Juan Paraiso (2003). *The Balete Book: A collection of demons, monsters and dwarfs from the Philippine lower mythology*. Philippines: Giraffe Books. ISBN 971-8832-79-3.

Chapter 22

Manananggal

The **Manananggal** (sometimes confused with the Wak Wak) is a vampire-like mythical creature of the Philippines, a malevolent, man-eating and blood-sucking monster or witch.

22.1 Mythology

The manananggal is described as hideous, scary, often depicted as female, and capable of severing its upper torso and sprouting huge bat-like wings to fly into the night in search of its victims. The word *manananggal* comes from the Tagalog word *tanggal* (cognate of Malay tanggal), which means "to remove" or "to separate", which literally translates as "remover" or "separator". In this case, "one who separates itself". The name also originates from an expression used for a severed torso.

The manananggal is said to favor preying on sleeping, pregnant women, using an elongated proboscis-like tongue to suck the hearts of fetuses, or the blood of someone who is sleeping. The severed lower torso is left standing, and is the more vulnerable of the two halves. Sprinkling salt, smearing crushed garlic or ash on top of the standing torso is fatal to the creature. The upper torso then would not be able to rejoin itself and would perish by sunrise.[1][2][3]

The myth of the Manananggal is popular in the Visayan region of the Philippines, especially in the western provinces of Capiz, Iloilo, and Antique. There are varying accounts of the features of a manananggal. Like vampires, Visayan folklore creatures, and aswangs, manananggals are also said to abhor garlic and salt.[4] They were also known to avoid daggers, light, vinegar, spices and the tail of a stingray, which can be fashioned as a whip.[2] Folklore of similar creatures can be found in the neighbouring nations of Indonesia and Malaysia. The province of Capiz is the subject or focus of many manananggal stories, as with the stories of other types of mythical creatures, such as ghosts, goblins, ghouls generically referred to as aswangs. Sightings are purported here, and certain local folk are said to believe in their existence despite modernization. The manananggal shares some features with the vampire of Balkan folklore, such as its dislike of garlic, salt, and vulnerability to sunlight.

22.2 Appearances in film and other media

- *Manananggal* (1927)

  First ever Filipino horror movie,[5][6] A silent picture movie portraying the manananggal in its current form, having the upper torso detach. Not much was known on the plot of the story.

  Cast: Mary Walter

  Directed: Jose Nepomuceno

- *Manananggal vs. Mangkukulam* (1960)[7]

Horror Comedy starring the top comedians of the 60's.

Directed by: Consuelo Osorio

cast: Pugo Lopito Patsy Chichay Aruray

Studios: Lea Productions (Prod. company)

- *Mga Bata ng Lagim* (1964)[7]

Star-studded cast of the 60's teen matinee idols "Sampaguita-VP All-Stars". A scene where German Moreno and Boy Alano turned into a manananggal after applying oil at their bodies after which they sang the popular paruparong bukid folksong.

cast: Sampaguita-VP All-Stars, German Moreno, Boy Alano

Directed by: Consuelo Osorio

- *Lipad, Darna, Lipad!* (1973)[8]

Gloria Romero plays as the respectable Miss Luna, Narda's school teacher who has a mysterious secret. She is the blood sucking flying creature that roams at night.

cast: Vilma Santos, Gloria Romero

Directed: Maning Borlaza

- *Pagsapit ng Dilim* (1975)[7]

Perla Bautista plays a mother who tricked her daughter Gina Pareno into becoming a manananggal as part of her coming of age rites.

cast: Perla Bautista, Gina Pareno

- *Shake, Rattle and Roll* (1984)

Herbert Bautista plays a teenager in a faraway province in an episode of this horror anthology movie series. A manananggal is said to live within the vicinity and is out to eat people. He is given the task by his grandmother to kill this creature. Having found a way to prevent it from returning to its body, he must now survive the night to protect his family from the creature's attacks.

Cast: Irma Alegre, Herbert Bautista, Mary Walter

Director: Peque Gallaga

- *Impaktita* (1989)

Jean Garcia plays the role of a young girl whose mother is a manananggal, and when she turns 18, she will transform into a wild bloodsucking creature at night by the eerie sound of a bat and sucks the blood of any living person she can find.

Cast: Jean Garcia, Richard Gomez, Aga Muhlach, Gloria Romero, Nida Blanca

- *Shake, Rattle & Roll IV* (1992)

A homeless family and their neighbors in the city of Manila are plagued by attacks from a manananggal. A little boy (IC Mendoza) suspects a nun (Aiko Melendez) to be that creature, but no one believes him. He finds himself racing to prove his suspicions before he becomes the monster's next victim.

- *Takot Ka Ba Sa Dilim?* (1996)

  A brief scene where Marjorie Barretto plays a young lass who turns into a ravenous manananggal at night who hunts for unsuspecting victims.

  Cast: Angelu de Leon, Rica Peralejo, Bobby Andrews, Marjorie Barretto, Red Sternberg, Amanda Page

- *Manananggal in Manila* (1997)

  An English-speaking manananggal Alma Concepcion spreads terror in Manila.

- *Krasue*, 2002 film by Bin Bunluerit

  based on krasue folklore

- *Dayo: Sa Mundo ng Elementalia*(2008)

  The plot revolves around Bubuy (Nash Aguas) who is out to save his abducted grandparents in the land of Elementalia.It features a friendly Vegetarian Manananggal named Anna (Katrina Legaspi), relating her to a different species of bat which is a fruit bat, as opposed the blood thirsty ones based on the folklore.[9]

  Cast: Nash Aguas, Katrina Legaspi, Pokwang

  Directed: Robert Quilao

- *Lose #3*, 2011 comic by Michael Deforge

  "Manananggal," a three page wordless comic.

- *Marvel Anime: Blade* (2011)

  Episode: 5 "Island Lights" (The Island of Fire)

  Blade and his partners encounter a mutated version of the Manananggal and its victims while hunting down Deacon Frost on the island of Siquijor, an island province in the Philippines.

- *The Aswang Phenomenon (Documentary)* (2011)

  Jordan Clark's documentary is an exploration of the aswang folklore and its effects on Philippine society. The evolution and history of the Manananggal is explored from an anthropological, sexual and pop culture view. Produced by High Banks Entertainment Ltd.[10]

  Cast: Peque Gallaga, Rodolfo Vera, Maricel Soriano

- *Aso ni San Roque (TV series)* (2012)

  Fatima is a blind girl with a golden heart who is the offspring of a mortal and a manananggal. Her fate is to end the devastation of the Aswang in the human world with the help of Anghel, the dog statue of San Roque that has miraculously animated. It features Kanlaon, the manananggal leader of the Aswang of the Wind (or Airborne aswangs). He once loved and failed to Lourdes, a manananggal herself and the mother of Fatima.

  Cast: Mona Louise Rey, LJ Reyes, Gardo Versoza

  Directed: Don Michael Perez

- *Supernatural: Fresh Meat by Alice Henderson* (Book) *(2013)*

A novel based on the tv series Supernatural features the main characters battling an Aswang in the Sierra Nevada mountains during a blizzard. The creature in this novel sucks human organs out through a proboscis and inserts body parts of other humans into the victim then seals the hole. The main characters make a whip tipped with a stingray barb and coated with spices to kill the creature.

- *Mananang Game (Android App)* (2014)

An android game based on the Manananggal wherein players fly through obstacles and avoid other hazards much like Flappy Bird.

Developer: *Jigzen Game Studios*

- *Elemento (TV series)* (2014)

Episode: Si Esperanza, Ang Rebeldeng Manananggal (Esperanza, The Rebel Manananggal)

The story is about Esperanza, played by(Glaiza de Castro), a pediatrician with two mortal sons. Her desire to protect her children and avoid the way of the life of being a manananggal.

Cast: Glaiza de Castro, Valerie Concepcion, Maria Isabel Lopez

Directed: Topel Lee

- *V/H/S (Film)* (2012)

22.3   Other terms and versions

- Aswang: Manananggals are popularly referred to as aswangs. However, *aswang* is a generic term and can refer to all types of ghouls, mananangals, witches (mangkukulam), etc.

- Tik-tik: Manananggals are sometimes referred to as tik-tik, the sound it makes while flying. Folklore dictates that the fainter the sound, the nearer the manananggal is. This is to confuse the victim. Black cats and crows often signal a tik-tik's presence, and deformed faces or bodies in children are allegedly signs of the aftermath of a tik-tik attack.

- Leyak

22.4   See also

- Philippine mythology

- Penanggalan - A vampire akin to Manananggal from the Malay peninsula

- Tiyanak - Blood-sucking creature in a form of a baby that turns into what is known to be the child of the devil

- Krasue - Floating vampiric female head and entrails that is similar to a manananggal

- Chonchon - Mapuche creature that also detaches its head

- Nukekubi - Japanese creature that also detaches its head to feed on victims

22.5 References

[1] Alip, Eufronio Melo (1950). *Political and Cultural History of the Philippines*. Philippines.

[2] Ramos, Maximo D. (1971). *Creatures of Philippine Lower Mythology*. Philippines: Phoenix Publishing. ISBN 971-06-0691-3.

[3] Bane, Theresa (2010). *Encyclopedia of Vampire Mythology*. USA: McFarland & Company, Inc. ISBN 978-0-7864-4452-6.

[4] Paraiso, Salvador; Jose Juan Paraiso (2003). *The Balete Book: A Collection of Demons, Monsters and Dwarfs from the Philippine Lower Mythology*. Philippines: Giraffe Books. ISBN 971-8832-79-3.

[5] "Early Pinoy Horror movies a compilation of classic Filipino movie video48.blogspot.com".

[6] Garcia, Jessie B. (2004). *A Movie Album Quizbook*. Iloilo City, Philippines: Erehwon Books & Magazine. ISBN 971-93297-0-X.

[7] "Manananggal vs Mangkukulam 1960".

[8] "LIPAD, DARNA, LIPAD (1973) http://pelikulaatbp.blogspot.com/".

[9] "Lea Salonga sings Dayo theme "Lipad" live (with video)".

[10] Clark, Jordan (2011) *The Aswang Phenomenon* High Banks Entertainment Ltd. https://www.youtube.com/watch?v=2ePhqoyLpXQ

22.6 Further reading

- Alip, Eufronio Melo (1950). *Political and Cultural History of the Philippines*. Philippines.

- Ramos, Maximo D. (1971). *Creatures of Philippine Lower Mythology*. Philippines: Phoenix Publishing. ISBN 971-06-0691-3.

- Eugenio, Damiana (2002). *Philippine Folk Literature: The Legends*. Philippines: University of the Philippines Press. p. 490. ISBN 971-542-357-4.

- Garcia, Jessie B. (2004). *A Movie Album Quizbook*. Iloilo City, Philippines: Erehwon Books & Magazine. ISBN 971-93297-0-X.

- Eugenio, Damiana (2007). *Philippine Folk Literature: An Anthology* (2nd ed.). Philippines: University of the Philippines Press. p. 498. ISBN 978-971-542-536-0.

- Bane, Theresa (2010). *Encyclopedia of Vampire Mythology*. USA: McFarland & Company, Inc. ISBN 978-0-7864-4452-6.

- Cruz, Neal (2008-10-31). "As I See It: Philippine mythological monsters". *Philippine Daily Inquirer*.

22.7 External links

- Filipino Folklore: Manananggal

- Mananang Game Official Website

Chapter 23

Manaul

The **Manaul** bird is a creature of Philippine mythology mentioned in the Code of Kalantiaw. According to this document, the killing of this bird is punishable by death. However, there is tale that the Manaul was the king of birds. He eventually became wicked and was turned into an bird as punishment. He was caught by the wind god, Tabluk Lani, but escaped. Homeless, the Manaul told the Sky that the Sea will rise until it covers it. The Manaul then tells the Sea that the Sky will push it down. Both were furious. The Sky began throwing giant rocks at the Sea which was creating giant waves. The Sky and Sea eventually stopped fighting but the rocks stayed on the sea and become the Manaul's home which are now the Philippine islands themselves. [1]

23.1 References

[1] Morrow, Paul. "The Fraudulent Legal Code of Kalantiaw". Retrieved 2008-06-20.

Chapter 24

Mangindusa

Mangindusa, is one of the four highly revered gods in the Tagbanua mythology, is also known as the "lord of the heavens."

Mangindusa dwells in a sacred area called **Awan-awan**, a place lying beyond the *langit*, in a region between the sky world and the earth. He lives with his wife **Bugawasin**, his messengers, and other celestial beings.

While Mangindusa is considered the highest-ranking deity, there is no traditional ascription to him as the sole "creator" of the world, although Christian mythology has had some influence in imbuing Mangindusa with more powers than he used to possess. In fact, the creation of the world and of human beings is said to have been the handiwork of the *diwata*.

Mangindusa has always been traditionally considered the punisher of *dusa* (crime). In Tagbanua society, the only recognized public dusa is *sumbang* (incest). In this case, Mangindusa holds the society responsible for the *sumbang*. Mangindusa's punishment of the society may take the form of withholding the rains. In the past, society punished the offenders by drowning them in the sea. In present society, a huge fine is imposed and in top of this a special *lumbay* ritual must given in honor of Mangindusa.[1]

24.1 References

[1] Tagabanua by Mark Joel Velasquez. Accessed August 28, 2008.

Chapter 25

Minokawa

Minokawa is a giant bird that belongs to the dragon family. Early people believed this creature is so big that it can swallow (or cover) the sun to explain the occurrence of eclipses.[1] It is even described as a giant bird named *Minokawa* that lives in outer space which can devour the sun and the moon, and would try to do the same with the earth.[2]

In a Bagobo tale, the *Minokawa* is a bird as large as an island. Its feathers are those of sharp swords, the eyes reflect like mirrors, its beak and legs are like steel. It lives "outside the sky, at the eastern horizon". While the Baua lived "above the sky" because the Visayans believe that there is a cave called "calulundan" above the sky, the entrance covered by blue smoke.[3]

25.1   Basic Legend

Before time began, very long ago, a great bird called *Minokawa* swallowed the moon. Seized with fear, all the people began to scream and made great noises. Then the bird peeped down to see what the matter was, and opened his mouth. But as soon as he opened his mouth, the moon sprang out and ran away.

The *Minokawa*-bird is as large as the Island of Negros or Bohol. It has a beak of steel, and his claws too are of steel. His eyes are mirrors, and each single feather is a sharp sword. He lives outside the sky, at the eastern horizon, ready to seize the moon and after the unsuccessful attempt of swallowing the satellite, it journeys and haunts again lurking under the earth.

The moon makes eight holes in the eastern horizon to come out of, and eight holes in the western horizon to go into, because every day the big bird tries to catch her, and she is afraid. The exact moment he tries to swallow her is just when she is about to come in through one of the holes in the east to shine on us again. If the *Minokawa* should swallow the moon, and the sun too, he would then come down to earth and gulp down men also. But when the moon is in the belly of the big bird, and the sky is dark, then all the Bagobo people will scream and cry, and beat gongs, because they fear they will all be eaten. Soon this racket makes the *Minokawa*-bird look down and "open his mouth to hear the sound." Then the moon jumps out of the bird's mouth and runs away.[4]

25.2   References

[1] "Da Adventure of Pendro Penduko". Retrieved 2008-10-09.

[2] "Minokawa (The Origin of the Eclipse)". Retrieved 2008-09-13.

[3] "THE DEMONS OF PHILIPPINE LOWER MYTHOLOGY". Archived from the original on 2009-10-24. Retrieved 2008-09-13.

[4] "Story of the Eclipse". Retrieved 2008-09-13.

Chapter 26

Nuno

For the Portuguese name see Nuno (given name)

A **nuno** (**duwende**) or **nuno sa punso** ("old man of the mound") is a dwarf-like creature in Philippine mythology. It is believed to live in an anthill or termite mound, hence its name, literally 'Ancestor/Grandparent living in the anthill'.

26.1 Description

The *nuno* is described to be a small old man with a long beard, and differs from a duwende or dwarf of Philippine folklore. The duwende is a playful hobgoblin who shows himself to children, while the *nuno* is a goblin easily angered and will do harm to those who damage or disturb his mound. If an invader destroys the nuno's home by kicking it, the offender's foot will become swollen. Nuno sa punso are also believed to inhabit places such as underneath large rocks, trees, riverbanks, caves, or a backyard.

26.2 Magical abilities

Nunos have the ability to curse trespassers. A curse may include the following:

- Swelling or pain on any part of the body

- Vomiting of blood

- Urinating black liquid

- Excessive hair growth on the back

In order for a nuno to successfully curse a person, the trespasser must come in close proximity of the nuno. If the trespasser is within range, the Nuno can spit on any part of the trespasser's body. The trespasser will then experience aches or soreness on the affected part of the body, such as stomach pains, swollen genitals (after urinating on the mound), or swollen feet (after kicking the mound).

26.3 Countermeasures against curses

There is a common belief that if modern medicine is unable to cure a particular illness, the ailment may be due to a *nuno*'s curse. The victim is brought to an *albularyo*, a Philippine practitioner of traditional medicine. The *albularyo* will perform a ceremony known as *tawas*. During this process, a piece of a candle is melted and the molten wax poured onto a disc or spoon. The molten wax is in turn poured into water. The image formed on the water will then be interpreted by the *albularyo*. The image aids in determining the cause of the patient's illness and where the curse actually happened.

In order to be cured, the victim's family may be asked to provide an offering to the nuno such as fruits or other food, drinks, or a material object. If the victim is still not healed after the offering, it may be necessary to personally ask the nuno's forgiveness, which is believed to be a wise measure, in order to prevent the permanent possession of the victim by an evil spirit, which could later cause the victim to become insane.

It is also possible to kill the nuno by catching it and crushing its head between a person's fingers or thighs. This will remove any spell cast by the nuno. But this method is not often recommended because it could evoke the wrath of a nuno's friends and relatives.

Legends also state that placing an obese or festively plump female on the side of a road after midnight will attract the nuno out of hiding, thus allowing those afflicted to seek their revenge on the goblin. The nuno has an odd affinity for large bodied mammals of the opposite sex.

26.4   Precautions

To avoid the wrath of a nuno sa Punso, children are reminded not to play outside between noon and three o'clock in the afternoon. They are also asked by their parents to come home before six o'clock in the evening. Children are also instructed avoid being noisy at places where nuno are believed to dwell. Children are also warned to ask permission or give fair notice before passing by such places inhabited by the nuno, which is done by saying *"tabi tabi po"* (literally *"please be on the side"* or *"please move aside"*, that is, you tell the nuno to stand aside), or "please let me pass by" or "I mean no harm as I pass through your territory, Old Man of the Mound".

26.5   Disrespect

Although most people respect the nuno and will abide by the many unwritten rules which serve the purpose of building a peaceful coexistence between human beings and nuno, some people still stubbornly choose not to. A disrespectful person will purposely trample around in tall grassy areas, places where nuno are also believed to inhabit. These people would also intentionally urinate on suspected nuno anthills to display dominance over the mound dweller.

26.6   Today

Since the 2005 introduction of the red imported fire ant in the Philippines, the legendary folk tale of the nuno has again become predominant.

26.7   References

- Tagalog-English Dictionary by Leo James English, Congregation of the Most Holy Redeemer, Manila, distributed by National Book Store, 1583 pages, ISBN 971-91055-0-X

- http://www.retrato.com.ph/photodtl.asp?id=SS00205

- http://www.everything2.com/index.pl?node_id=1066706

- http://www.imdb.com/title/tt0787100/

- http://www.language.berkeley.edu/ucfcp/unit5/gawain.php

Chapter 27

Philippine mythical creatures

Main article: Philippine mythology

Philippine folklore, unlike Greek or Roman mythologies, has not been organized into a formal pantheon, does not generally contain long epics, nor has it been relegated to history. To this day, Philippine myths still have an active role in the lives of rural Filipinos. The countless myths circulating throughout the Filipino countryside contain a large variety of **mythical creatures**. Although there is no scientific evidence for any of these creatures, there is also no shortage in the rural parts of the Philippines of people who believe firmly in their existence. This discrepancy is sometimes rationalized by the explanation that only pure and good mortals are able to see these creatures.

27.1 List of Philippine Mythical Creatures

27.1.1 Bungisngis

Main article: Bungisngis

Bungisngis is a one-eyed giant. This Philippine folklore giant lives in forest and woods. It is a happy and a playful cyclops. It is also commonly known as 'Mahentoy' in the northern part of Davao.

27.1.2 Aswang

Main article: Aswang

Aswangs are shapeshifters. They are human-like by day but transform into different monstrous forms to harass and eat awake humans at night, especially pregnant women who are about to give birth.[1] Aswangs can change from a human to an animal form, usually as a bat, a cat, a pig or a black dog. Some aswangs can change form at will, others through the use of foul oils concocted by evil magicians. Aswangs appear at night to prey upon unwary travelers or sleeping people. It is said that they have a peculiar liking for the taste of human liver. The myth of the Aswang is popular in the Visayas, especially in provinces such as Capiz, Antique, and Iloilo. Aswangs also have a peculiar liking for the fetus of pregnant women and are said to find their quarry by the scent of the mother, which to the aswang smells like ripe jackfruit. Upon finding the house of the pregnant mother, the aswang alights on the roof from where it stretches its tongue until it is as thin as a thread and uses it to enter the womb and feast on the fetus.

Bathala *(top), a* diwata *(bottom), and the* Sarimanok *(center).*

27.1.3   Bathala

Main article: Bathala

Bathala, *Diyos* or *Apo* it is the creation god in Filipino myths.[1][2][3]

27.1.4   Berberoka

Main article: Berberoka

Berberoka ensnares its victims by drinking enough water in the pond until a number of fish appear into the surface.

27.1.5   Diwata

Main article: Diwata

Diwata (from Sanskrit **devada**, "*gods*"), *engkantada* (from Spanish: **encantada**, "*enchantress, charmed*") or engkanto (from Spanish: **encanto**, *"spell, incantation, charm"*) are dryads who guard natural creations such as forests, seas, mountains, land and air.[1] *Diwata*s are said to reside in large trees, such as acacia and balete. They bring blessings or curses upon those who do good or harm to the forests and mountains. One famous diwata is Maria Makiling, guardian of Mount Makiling in Laguna province. *Engkanto* (sometimes spelled *Encanto*) is an umbrella term for most supernatural beings. The common connotation is that they are fairies who reside primarily in the forests and the sea. They can also be called encantado (male) or encantada (female).

27.1.6   Duwende

Main article: Duende (mythology)

Duwende are goblins, hobgoblins, elves or dwarfs (*Spanish*: *duende* "*goblin, elf, charm*" < "*duen de (casa)*", *owner of the house*). They are little creatures who can provide good fortune or bad fate to humans.[1] In the Philippines, duwendes frequently live in houses, in trees, underground, termite like mound or hill, and in rural areas. They are known to be either good or mischievous, depending on how homeowners treat them. They usually come out at 12 noon for an hour and during the night. Filipinos always mutter words ("tabi-tabi po" or "bari-bari apo ma ka ilabas kami apo") asking them to excuse themselves for bothering the Duwendes. Filipinos would leave food on the floor, so that the duwende residing (or guarding) the house would not be angry with them. They also take your things,and laugh at you when you try to find it. They give it back when they feel like it,or when you tell them to please give it back.

27.1.7   Ekek

Ekek are creatures who are bird-like humans. They are winged-humans who at night search for victims. They hunger for flesh and blood. It is like a Harpy.

27.1.8   Kapre

Main article: Kapre

Kapre is a filthy giant[1] who likes to smoke huge rolls of cigars, and hide within, and atop large trees, particularly the balete and old acacia or mango trees. A Filipino bigfoot, it scares away little children who play at night.[4] If you're stuck in a place and you keep going around in circles, you said to be played around with by a Kapre. To escape its control, you must remove your shirt/clothing, and wear it inside-out.

27.1.9 Malakas and Maganda

Malakas *and* Maganda.

Malakas and Maganda (literally, *Strong One* and *Beautiful One*) are Filipino versions of Adam and Eve. They are said to have sprung from a large bamboo tree pecked by a Sarimanok known as Magaulancealabarca.[2][5][6]

27.1.10   Mambabarang

Mambabarang (summoner) is a witch who uses insects and spirits to enter the body of any person they hate. A *Mambabarang* is a kind of a mangkukulam. Mambabarangs are ordinary human beings with black magic who torture and later kill their victims by infesting their bodies with insects. They are different from Mangkukulams - the latter only inflict pain or illness. Mambabarangs use a strand of hair from their chosen victim and tie it to the bugs or worms which they will use as a medium. When they prick the bug, the victim immediately experiences the intended effect.

27.1.11   Manananggal

Main article: Manananggal

Manananggal is an *aswang* that can fly after separating itself from the lower half of its body. It eats babies and fetuses from a mothers womb. It eats babies by means of passing their long tongue through a small hole from the roof of a house. The sharp end of the tongue touches the mother's navel to suck the blood of the fetus or unborn child.[7] This creature's name was derived from the Filipino word, *tanggal*, which means "to separate" because of the manananggal's ability to separate itself from its lower body.[1]

A *manananggal* can also be a sorceress that visits villages and barrios. To feed, the self-segmenter chooses an isolated place where she will leave her lower torso while she hunts at night. When she separates from her lower torso, she then gains her ability to fly. She then goes off in search of houses where pregnant women reside. Upon choosing a suitable victim, the Manananggal alights on the house and inserts her tongue through the roof. The tongue is long, hollow and extremely flexible. She uses it to puncture the womb of the sleeping woman and to suck out the fetus. At other times, she seduces men with her beauty and lures them to a private place before eating them alive. She usually eats the insides, like the heart, stomach or the liver. Sunlight is deadly to the Manananggal when she is in her monstrous form. Should her two halves still be separate with the coming of dawn, she will be destroyed. According to legend, to destroy the Manananggal, one should search for the lower torso that she leaves behind during her nightly hunts. Salt, ash, and/or garlic should then be placed on the exposed flesh, preventing the monster from combining again and leaving it vulnerable to sunlight. Small containers of salt, ash and raw rice, and the smell of burning rubber are said to deter the Manananggal from approaching one's house.

27.1.12   Manaul

The *manaul* is a mythical king who became a bird. He was believed to have caused the seas and the skies to fight against each other. The clash between the seas and skies resulted to the formation of the Philippine islands.

27.1.13   Mangkukulam

Main article: Mangkukulam

Mangkukulam or *bruha* (from Spanish: **bruja**, "witch") are witches, wizards, *bruho* (Spanish:**brujo**, "*wizard, male witch*"), or sorcerers who cast evil spells to humans. This bewitcher is also called *manggagaway*.[1] The *Mangkukulam* uses dark magic.

The difference between a *mambabarang* and a *mangkukulam* is that the *mambabarang* uses magical insects to bring harm to his victims. These insects are released after incantations, when they will search for their supposed victim and burrow under the skin, impregnating her. After some time, matruculans return to the house to kill the pregnant mother, open her abdomen, and eat the growing fetus.

A manananggal.

Maria Makiling.

27.1.14 Maria Makiling

Main article: Maria Makiling

Mariang Makiling is a fairy who dwells atop Laguna's Mount Makiling, an inactive volcano. Oral tradition described that Mount Makiling was once a castle and Mariang Makiling was a princess who fell in love with a mortal.

27.1.15 Multo

Multo, the Tagalog word for ghost, comes from the Spanish word *muerto*, which means "dead". Superstitious Filipinos believe that some kind of multo, often a spirit of their former kin, regularly visits them.

27.1.16 Nuno sa punso

Main article: Nuno sa punso

Nuno sa punso (literally, *goblin of the mound*) are goblins or elves who live within mysterious lumps of soil (ant hills). They can provide a person who steps on their shelter with good luck or misfortune.[1] Superstitious Filipinos, when passing by a mound, will ask the resident nuno's permission to let them pass with the phrase, *"Tabi-tabi po"*. Strange and sudden illnesses that befall a person are sometimes attributed to nunos. It is also said that nunos don't like being pointed at, and could cause you to break your finger.

27.1.17 Pasatsat

Pasatsat is word rooted on the Pangasinense word *satsat*, meaning "to stab". *Pasatsats* are ghosts of people who died or were killed in the Second World War. Coffins during the time were so expensive, so the families of the dead wrapped the corpses in reed mats or *icamen*. The dead were buried in places other than cemeteries because tomb robberies were rampant during that era of extreme poverty. These ghosts usually show up in solitary paths and block passersby. To get rid of such a ghost, one needs to stab (hence *pasatsat*) the reed mat and unravel it, but doing so will show no presence of a corpse, although the mat will emit a noxious odor, much like that of putrid flesh.

27.1.18 Santelmo

Main article: St. Elmo's Fire

Santelmo, or *Santo Elmo*, is a fireball seen by dozens of Filipinos, especially those living in the Sierra Madre Mountains. It was scientifically explained as electric fields which have diverged from the lines. However, the sightings were reported since the Spanish era (16th-19th centuries). (See also *Shinen* and *Will-o-Wisps*) There were also sightings in the Alps and Himalayas.

27.1.19 Sarangay

Sarangay, is a creature resembling a bull with a huge muscular body and a jewel attached to its ears.

27.1.20 Sarimanok

Main article: Sarimanok

A *Sarimanok* is a magical, mythical bird who brings good luck to anyone who are able to catch it. A Sarimanok known as Magaul is associated with the legend of Malakas and Maganda. Magaul was the Sarimanok bird that pecked the bamboo from where Malakas and Maganda were born from.[2][5][6]

The Sarimanok.

27.1.21   Sirena

Main articles: Dyesebel and Sirena (Philippine Mythology)
 Sirena is a mermaid, a sea creature with a human upper body and a fish tail instead of lower extremities. They attract fishermen and tourists.[1] Sirenas are reportedly often seen ashore by fishermen, especially in the towns bordering the Pacific Ocean.

27.1.22   Siyokoy

Main article: Siyokoy (Philippine Mythology)

Siyokoy are mermen, sea creatures that have a human form and scaled bodies. The *Siyokoy* is the male counterpart of the Sirena. The lower extremities of a Philippine merman can either be a fishtail or scaled legs and webbed feet. They could also have long, green tentacles. They drown mortals for food. Siyokoys have gill slits, are colored brown or green, and have scaly skin, comparable to that of a fish.

Dyesebel, *a Philippine mermaid.*

27.1.23 Tikbalang

Main article: Tikbalang

Tikbalang or *tigbalang* (demon horse) is a half-man and half-horse creature. It has a horse's head, the body of a human but with the feet of the horse. It travels at night to rape female mortals. The raped women will then give birth to more *tikbalang*. They are also believed to cause travelers to lose their way particularly in mountainous or forest areas.[1] Tikbalangs are very playful with people, and they usually make a person imagine things that aren't real. Sometimes a Tikbalang will drive a person crazy. Legends say that when rain falls while the sun is shining, a pair of *Tikbalangs* are being wed. Since horses only arrived in the Philippine archipelago during the Spanish colonization (thus, the borrowed term 'kabayo'), there is a theory that the image of a half-horse, half-man creature was propagated by the conquistadors to keep the natives afraid of the night. There are stories claiming that the *Tikbalang* are actually half-bird, half-man creatures, much like the Japanese tengu.

27.1.24 Tiyanak

Main article: Tiyanak

Tiyanak are babies who died before receiving baptism rites. After death, they go to a place known as Limbo, a chamber of Hell which unbaptized dead people fall into, and are transformed into evil spirits. These phantasms return into the mortal realm in the form of goblins to eat living victims. The *tiyanak* can also be the offspring of a woman and a demon. It can also be an aborted fetus which comes back to take revenge on its mother. Most Tiyanaks are said to live in forests. If they see a human, they transform into what looks like a normal baby. When the person notices the Tiyanak and comes near to take a look at it, the Tiyanak changes back to its true form and eats its prey. And since they often seen coming out of trees it may also refer to Tboli legends, Tibolis are known for hanging their infants in trees who died after birth.

27.1.25 Wakwak

Main article: Wakwak

Wakwak is assumed to grab humans at night as its prey, just like Manananggal and the Ekek who can fly. It likes to haunt in the rural areas of the Philippines. The Wakwak has no ability to separate its torso from its body. Some people believed that it is a night bird that belongs to a witch.

The Wakwak makes a sound by flapping its wings whilst flying. The sound that it produced is typically linked to the presence of an Unglu (vampire) or Ungo (ghost or monster). The Wakwak's sound also indicates that it is searching for victims. When the sound is loud, it means that it is far from you. If not, then it is near you and ready to attack. The Wakwak rips and maims its victims and then feeds on their hearts. The old folks described the Wakwak as creatures with long sharp talons and a pair of wings just like bats. Its talons or claws are used in slashing its victims in order to retrieve their hearts.

27.2 References

27.2.1 Specific

[1] "Tagalog-English Dictionary by Leo James English, Congregation of the Most Holy Redeemer, Manila, distributed by National Book Store, 1583 pages, ISBN 971-91055-0-X

[2] Malakas at Maganda Legend, Bambooman.com, 2006, retrieved on August 5, 2007

[3] Giovanni, R.C. The Origins of Man, Ancient Mythology, Children of Pearl, Geocities.com (undated), retrieved on: August 5, 2007

A Tikbalang.

[4] The Kapre, Ancient Mythology, Children of the Pearl, Geocities.com (undated), retrieved on August 5, 2007

[5] The Tale of Malakas and Maganda, Ancient Mythology, Children of the Pearl, Geocities.com (undated), retrieved on August 5, 2007

[6] Story of Malakas and Maganda, Everything2.com, retrieved on: August 5, 2007

[7] The Manananggal, Ancient Mythology, Children of the Pearl, Geocities.com (undated), retrieved on August 5, 2007

27.2.2 General

- Young, Johnny. Philippine Myths and Legends and Tanikalang Ginto, the Philippines' Web Directory, June 23, 2003, retrieved on July 29, 2007

- Cole, Mabel Cook. Philippine Folk Tales, Chicago, 1916 and APSIS Editor Johann Stockinger, November 1, 1997 retrieved on: July 29, 2007

- Magical Creatures and Non-human Beings of the Philippines, retrieved on: July 29, 2007

- Contemporary Illustrations of *Tikbalang* (demon horse), *Mambabarang* (summoner) and *Diwata* (goddess), retrieved on: July 30, 2007

27.3 External links

- Image of Malakas and Maganda by Nestor Redondo from *Men, Maiden and Myths*, Shanes and Shanes (1979), Art Gallery at alanguilan.com

- Filipino Folklore: Dwende

Chapter 28

Philippine mythology

Philippine mythology include a collection of tales and superstitions about magical creatures and entities. Many Filipinos, even though heavily Christianized, still believe in these tales. The prevalence of belief in the figures of Filipino mythology is strong in the provinces.

Because the country has many islands and is inhabited by different ethnic groups, Philippine mythology and superstitions are very diverse. However, certain similarities exist among these groups, such as the belief in Heaven (*kaluwalhatian*, *kalangitan*, *kamurawayan*), Hell (*impiyerno*, *kasamaan*), and the human soul (*kaluluwa*).

28.1 Philippine folk literature

Main article: Philippine folk literature

Philippine mythology is derived from Philippine folk literature, which is the traditional oral literature of the Filipino people. This refers to a wide range of material due to the ethnic mix of the Philippines. Each unique ethnic group has its own stories and myths to tell.

While the *oral* and thus *changeable* aspect of folk literature is an important defining characteristic, much of this oral tradition had been written into a print format. To point out that folklore in a written form can still be considered folklore, Utely pointed out that folklore "may appear in print, but must not freeze into print."[1] It should be pointed out that all the examples of folk literature cited in this article are taken from print, rather than oral sources.

University of the Philippines professor, Damiana Eugenio, classified Philippines Folk Literature into three major groups: folk narratives, folk speech, and folk songs.[2] Folk narratives can either be in prose: the myth, the *alamat* (legend), and the *kuwentong bayan* (folktale), or in verse, as in the case of the folk epic. Folk speech includes the *bugtong* (riddle) and the *salawikain* (proverbs). Folk songs that can be sub-classified into those that tell a story (folk ballads) are a relative rarity in Philippine folk literature. These form the bulk of the Philippines' rich heritage of folk songs.

28.2 Philippine pantheon

Main article: Deities of Philippine mythology

The stories of ancient Philippine mythology include deities, creation stories, mythical creatures, and beliefs. Ancient Philippine mythology varies among the many indigenous tribes of the Philippines. Some groups during the pre-Spanish conquest era believed in a single Supreme Being who created the world and everything in it, while others chose to worship a multitude of tree and forest deities (*diwatas*). *Diwata*s came from the Sanskrit word *devata* which means "deity", one of the several significant Hindu influences in the Pre-Hispanic religion of the ancient Filipinos. Below are some of the

58

gods and goddesses of the ancient Philippines:

Ancient Tagalog Deities:

- **Bathala**- the chief deity of the Tagalogs.

- **Lakampati (Lacapati/Lacanpate)** - the major fertility deity of the ancient Tagalogs. Farmers with their children brought offerings for her/him at the fields and invoke her/him to protect them from famine. Some sources also said that foods and words are offered to her/him by her/his devotees asking for "water" for their fields and "fish" when they set sail in the sea for fishing. Lakampati was a hermaphrodite deity. S/he is identified to the ancient Zambal goddess Ikapati although s/he also has a characteristics similar to other Zambal deities such as Anitong Tawo, Dumangan, Damulag, Kalasokus, and Kalaskas. S/he is the mother of Anagolay and wife of Mapulon. In some myths, s/he is listed as the wife of Bathala himself, before the world was created.

- **Pati** - According to Ferdinand Blumentritt the Igorots call the rain Pati and look upon him as a merciful divinity to whom they directed their prayers. According to Dr. D. Sinibaldo Mas, the anito of the rain is called Pati by the Ifugaos.

- **Lakambakod (Lachan Bacor)** – a phallic god who was the protector of the growing crops and healer of diseases. His name literally means "great/noble fence", from Lakan (a title of nobility) + bakod (fence) according to Diksyunaryo-Tesauro Pilipino-Ingles by J.V. Panganiban. Some sources claim him to be a protector of houses. One of his identifiers is his penis, which was said to be as long as a rice stalk.

- **Idiyanale (Idianale)** – the goddess of labor and good deeds. Natives used to call for her guidance in order to make their works successful. She married the agricultural god Dimangan and had two offspring.

- **Amansinaya (Aman Sinaya)** – the patron goddess of fishermen, she was appealed when the fishing net were cast. She is identified as one of the primordial deities of creation, existing alongside Bathala and Amihan during the creation of land.

- **Amanikable (Ama ni Cable/Ama ni Coable)** – the patron god of hunters. Sometimes identified as the god of the sea, known for his ill and frightful temper.

- **Diyan Masalanta (Dian Masalanta)** – The goddess of love, fecundity and childbirth. Daughter of Anagolay and Dumakulem.

- **Apolaki (Apolaqui)** – the ancient Pangasinenses worshipped him as their supreme deity addressed as Ama-Gaoley or Anagaoley(Supreme Father) whom they invoke for various matters such as war, trade and travel. They offered oils, incenses, and other aromatic herbs to his idol/images, slaves and pigs was also sacrificed in his honor. He was Identified to Suku a deity of ancient Kapampangans which associated him to the sun. Based on historical records, there is no hard evidence that he was also worshiped by the ancient Tagalogs, he is often not listed (just like Mayari) to the pantheon of anitos that ancient Tagalogs worshiped. In some informal and modern folktale version based on Pampangan Mythology his sister was Mayari a Zambal deity and their father was Bathala which is a Tagalog deity, this probably caused the misconception. Some sources list him as the son of Bathala and brother of Hanan, Mayari and Tala, but other sources list him as the son of Anagolay and Dumakulem, brother of Diyan Masalanta.

- **Mayari/Malyari (Mallari)** – She/He was worshipped by the Negritos of Zambales as their chief deity in which the "bayoc" (high priest) was the only one allowed to make offerings and sacrifices to him/her. Mayari seems to be the only one represented by an actual idol among the Zambal pantheon, a wooden head with a straw body and arms, constructed and clothed by the bayoc for the occasion. Based on historical records, there is no hard evidence that she/he was also worshiped by the ancient Tagalogs, so as Anitong Tawo and Dumangan. In Pampangan mythology he/she was a sibling of Suku, he/she was also associated to the moon based on that mythology, in some informal and modern folktale version based on the said myth his/her brother was Apolaki a Pangasinense deity and their father was Bathala which is a Tagalog deity, this probably caused the misconception. The ancient Tagalogs do venerate the moon, however there is no recorded evidence that they deified it as Mayari. She was considered the most beautiful of all the gods.

- **Lakambini (Lacambui)** – An obscure deity often called by the Spaniards as "abogado de la garganta" (the throat advocate). It is also known as the pure maiden.

- **Mangkukutod (Mancucutor)** – the patron god of a particular class of ancient Tagalogs, but the traditions were very obscure.

- **Anitong Tawo (Aniton Tavo)** – the god of the wind and of rain of the ancient Zambal. The name literally means "man god or demigod". He received the most important sacrifices among the deities invoked for good crops.

- **Kabunian** - One of the gods to some tribes (Ibaloi, Kalanguya, Kankana-ey) in the cordillera mountain range, specially in Benguet Province. **Benguet Kankana-eys** - Many years ago, some old folks believed that he resides in Mt. Kabunian (in Bakun, Benguet) while Ibaloi and Kalanguya believers say he resides in Mt. Pulag (straddling the boundaries of Benguet and Ifugao) together with the spirits of their ancestors and anitos.

- **Ginoong Ganay (Unmarried Lady)** - according to Luciano P.R. Santiago (To Love and to Suffer) the goddess who was believed to inhabit the "calumpang tree" was the advocate of single women. Her presence in the tree was heralded by the fact that its pretty flowers drove away their insect suitors by releasing a rank scent.

28.3   Creation myths

There are many different creation myths in Philippine mythology, originating from various ethnic groups.

28.3.1   The Story of Bathala

In the beginning of time there were three powerful gods who lived in the universe. Bathala was the caretaker of the earth, Ulilang Kaluluwa (*lit. Orphaned Spirit*), a huge serpent who lived in the clouds, and Galang Kaluluwa (*lit. Wandering spirit*), the winged god who loves to travel. These three gods did not know each other.

Bathala often dreamt of creating mortals but the empty earth stops him from doing so. Ulilang Kaluluwa who was equally lonely as Bathala, liked to visit places and the earth was his favorite. One day the two gods met. Ulilang Kaluluwa, seeing another god rivalling him, was not pleased. He challenged Bathala to a fight to decide who would be the ruler of the universe. After three days and three nights, Ulilang Kaluluwa was slain by Bathala. Instead of giving him a proper burial, Bathala burned the snake's remains. A few years later the third god, Galang Kaluluwa, wandered into Bathala's home. He welcomed the winged god with much kindness and even invited him to live in his kingdom. They became true friends and were very happy for many years.

Galang Kaluluwa became very ill. Before he died he instructed Bathala to bury him on the spot where Ulilang Kaluluwa's body was burned. Bathala did exactly as he was told. Out of the grave of the two dead gods grew a tall tree with a big round nut, which is the coconut tree. Bathala took the nut and husked it. He noticed that the inner skin was hard. The nut itself reminded him of Galang Kaluluwa's head. It had two eyes, a nose, and a round mouth. Its leaves looked so much like the wings of his dear winged friend. But the trunk was hard and ugly, like the body of his enemy, the snake Ulilang Kaluluwa.

Bathala realized that he was ready to create the creatures he wanted with him on earth. He created the vegetation, animals, and the first man and woman. Bathala built a house for them out of the trunk and leaves of the coconut' trees. For food, they drank the coconut juice and ate its delicious white meat. Its leaves, they discovered, were great for making mats, hats, and brooms. Its fiber could be used for rope and many other things.

28.3.2 Visayan version

This is an ancient Visayan account of creation:

Thousands of years ago, there was no land, sun, moon, or stars, and the world was only a great sea of water, above which stretched the sky. The water was the kingdom of the god Maguayan, and the sky was ruled by the great god, Kaptan.

Maguayan had a daughter called Lidagat, the sea, and Kaptan had a son known as Lihangin, the wind. The gods agreed to the marriage of their children, so the sea became the bride of the wind.

A daughter and three sons were born to them. The sons were called Likalibutan, Liadlao, and Libulan, and the daughter received the name of Lisuga.

Likalibutan had a body of rock and was strong and brave; Liadlao was formed of gold and was always happy; Libulan was made of copper and was weak and timid; and the beautiful Lisuga had a body of pure silver and was sweet and gentle. Their parents were very fond of them, and nothing was wanting to make them happy.

After a time Lihangin died and left the control of the winds to his eldest son Likalibutan. The faithful wife Lidagat soon followed her husband, and the children, now grown up, were left without father or mother. However, their grandfathers, Kaptan and Maguayan, took care of them and guarded them from all evil.

After some time, Likalibutan, proud of his power over the winds, resolved to gain more power, and asked his brothers to join him in an attack on Kaptan in the sky above. They refused at first, but when Likalibutan became angry with them, the amiable Liadlao, not wishing to offend his brother, agreed to help. Then together they induced the timid Libulan to join in the plan.

When all was ready, the three brothers rushed at the sky, but they could not beat down the gates of steel that guarded the entrance. Likalibutan let loose the strongest winds and blew the bars in every direction. The brothers rushed into the opening, but were met by the angry god Kaptan. So terrible did he look that they turned and ran in terror, but Kaptan, furious at the destruction of his gates, sent three bolts of lightning after them.

The first struck the copper Libulan and melted him into a ball. The second struck the golden Liadlao and he too was melted. The third bolt struck Likalibutan and his rocky body broke into many pieces and fell into the sea. So huge was he that parts of his body stuck out above the water and became what is known as land.

In the meantime the gentle Lisuga had missed her brothers and started to look for them. She went toward the sky, but as she approached the broken gates, Kaptan, blind with anger, struck her too with lightning, and her silver body broke into thousands of pieces.

Kaptan then came down from the sky and tore the sea apart, calling on Maguayan to come to him and accusing him of ordering the attack on the sky. Soon Maguayan appeared and answered that he knew nothing of the plot as he had been asleep deep in the sea. After some time, he succeeded in calming the angry Kaptan. Together they wept at the loss of their grandchildren, especially the gentle and beautiful Lisuga, but even with their powers, they could not restore the dead back to life. However, they gave to each body a beautiful light that will shine forever.

And so it was the golden Liadlao who became the sun and the copper Libulan, the moon, while Lisuga's pieces of silver were turned into the stars of heaven. To wicked Likalibutan, the gods gave no light, but resolved to make his body support a new race of people. So Kaptan gave Maguayan a seed and he planted it on one of the islands.

Soon a bamboo tree grew up, and from the hollow of one of its branches, a man and a woman came out. The man's name was Sikalak and the woman was called Sikabay. They were the parents of the human race. Their first child was a son whom they called Libo; afterwards they had a daughter who was known as Saman.

Pandaguan, the youngest son, was very clever and invented a trap to catch fish. The very first thing he caught was a huge shark. When he brought it to land, it looked so great and fierce that he thought it was surely a god, and he at once ordered his people to worship it. Soon all gathered around and began to sing and pray to the shark. Suddenly the sky and sea opened, and the gods came out and ordered Pandaguan to throw the shark back into the sea and to worship none, but them.

All were afraid except Pandaguan. He grew very bold and answered that the shark was as big as the gods, and that since he had been able to overpower it he would also be able to conquer the gods. Then Kaptan, hearing this, struck Pandaguan with a small lightning bolt, for he did not wish to kill him but merely to teach him a lesson. Then he and Maguayan decided to punish these people by scattering them over the earth, so they carried some to one land and some to another. Many children were afterwards born, and thus the earth became inhabited in all parts.

Pandaguan did not die. After lying on the ground for thirty days he regained his strength, but his body was blackened from the lightning, and his descendants became the dark-skinned tribe, the Negritos.

As punishment, his eldest son, Aryon, was taken north where the cold took away his senses. While Libo and Saman were carried south, where the hot sun scorched their bodies. A son of Saman and a daughter of Sikalak were carried east, where the land at first was so lacking in food that they were compelled to eat clay.

28.3.3 The legend of Maria Makiling

Main article: Maria Makiling

Maria Makiling is a diwata (fairy or forest nymph) who takes care of the ecologically rich Mount Makiling,[3] a dormant volcano in Laguna, Philippines. She is considered the protector of the mountain and the forests that surround it. She is also considered one of the most widely known diwata in Philippine Mythology. While many legends and superstitions exist about her, many share the common theme of a beautiful woman who falls in love with a man.

28.3.4 The legend of Minggan

Main articles: Minggan and Mariang Sinukuan

Minggan is a giant lived alone in Sierra Madre Mountain ranges and was in love with Mariang Sinukuan, the mountain spirit goddess. From time to time, Minggan would climb the mountains and offer her gigantic fruits and vegetables such as potatoes the size of boulders, which he transported in a huge wheel barrow. One day, Mariang Sinukuan told Minggan that he could only win her heart if he passed a test. "I want you to stop the river from flowing, I want you to build a pond in the mountains so I can be with all the living things that lived under water." The task could only be done if Minggan could carry enormous boulders of rocks from the surrounding mountains and throw them to the great river. The goddess added a condition. The task should be completed before daybreak. Minggan turned when he heard the rooster. He saw Mariang Sinukuan and realized that he had failed the test.

Elito Circa (*a famous Filipino folk artist*) had heard of this legend. His father and grandfather used to tell him that the giant`s footprints could still be found in Palayupay in Pantabangan. He heard from his folks how in some parts of the mountain, Minggan`s wheel barrow had left marks in the trunks of trees.

28.4 Mythological creatures, demons and monsters

Main article: Philippine mythical creatures

The *Aswang* [4] is a generic term for all types of ghouls (an eater of the dead), vampires, and werewolf and other malevolent creatures described from hereon. The (*Agta*) is a black tree spirit or man. The *Dila* (The Tongue), is a spirit that passes through the bamboo flooring of provincial houses, then licks the victims to death.. Other mythical creatures include fairies (*Diwata*), dryads (*Engkanto*), dwarves (*Duwende*), tree-residing trolls (*Kapre*), self-segmenting vampire and the most stereotyped 'Aswang' (*Manananggal*), witches or warlocks (*Mangkukulam*/Manggagamot), spirit-summoners (*Mambabarang*), goblins (*Nuno sa Punso*), ghosts (*Multo*), fireballs (*Santelmo*), mermaids (*Serena*), mermen (*Siyokoy*), demon-horses (*Tikbalang*), evil spirits (*Hantu Demon*), demon-infants (*Tiyanak*), Moon-eater (*Bakunawa*), *a dragon which has been tempted by the beauty of the seven moons, he was punished by Bathala(GOD) after eating the second to the last moon, and the (*Wakwak*) or night birds belonging to a witch or vampire or the witch or vampire itself in the form of a night bird.*

28.5 References

28.5.1 Specific

[1] Utely, Francis Lee. "A Definition of Folklore," American Folklore, Voice of America Forum Lectures, ed. Tristram Coffin, III 1968, p14.

[2] Eugenio, Damiana (2007). Philippine Folk Literature: An Anthology, 2nd, Quezon City: University of the Philippines Press, 498. ISBN 978-971-542-536-0.

[3] "Philippine Daily Inquirer". Financial Times Ltd. Philippine Daily Inquirer. Feb 21, 2009.

[4] Filipino Creatures of the Night

28.5.2 General

- Barangay-Sixteenth Century Philippine Culture and Society by William Henry Scott

- Philippine Folklore Stories by John Maurice Miller

28.6 External links

- SurLaLune Fairy Tales: Philippine Folk Tales by Mabel Cook Cole

- Image of Malakas and Maganda by Nestor Redondo from *Men, Maiden and Myths*, Shanes and Shanes (1979), Art Gallery at alanguilan.com

- Aswang - Pinoy Supernatural Creatures

Chapter 29

Pugot

The **Pugot** ("decapitated one") is a mythical fiend that is found in the Ilocos region.[1] It can assume various shapes such as hogs, dogs or even as humans. However, it usually appears as a black, gigantic headless being. The creature usually resides in dark places or deserted houses. However, they especially like living in trees such as the *duhat* (*Eugenia cumini*), *santol* (*Sandoricum koetjape*), and tamarind. [2]

Aside from its shapeshifting abilities, the *pugot* can also move at great speeds, feeding on snakes and insects that it finds among the trees. It feeds by thrusting food through its neck stump.[2]

Although terrifying, the *pugot* is relatively harmless. However, the creature is fond of women's underwear and steals them while they are being dried on a clothesline.[1]

The *pugot* is also found in the Ifugao myth "Tulud Nimputul: The Self-Beheaded" where he appears to the human hero. He was fed by the hero with chopped chicken meat that was mixed with blood.[2]

29.1   References

[1] Paraiso, Salvador; Jose Juan Paraiso (2003). *The Balete Book: A collection of demons, monsters and dwarfs from the Philippine lower mythology*. Philippines: Giraffe Books. ISBN 971-8832-79-3.

[2] Ramos, Maximo D. (1971). *Creatures of Philippine Lower Mythology*. Philippines: University of the Philippines Press.

Chapter 30

Santelmo

For other uses, see St. Elmo (disambiguation) and San Telmo (disambiguation).

The **Santelmo** (**St. Elmo's Fire**) is a creature of Philippine mythology. The term *santelmo* is the shortened form of the Tagalog words "Apoy ni San Elmo "-"St. Elmo's Fire". St. Elmo's Fire has long served as an omen of heavenly intervention to sailors. The ancient Greeks termed a single jet of the fire, Helena, and a double jet, Castor and Pollux. It has also been known by the names St. Nicholas and St. Hermes, corpusante and Corpus Santos. The name of St. Elmo is attributed to an Italian derivation of Sant 'Ermo or St. Erasmus (circa 300), the patron saint of the early Mediterranean sailors challenging the powers of storm and sea in small sailing vessels.[1]

30.1 Physical Appearance

St. Elmo's Fires have ranged from a ghostly dancing flame to natural fireworks. It usually is of a blue or bluish-white colour attached to fixed, grounded conductors and has a lifetime of minutes. The flame is heatless and non-consuming, occasionally accompanied by a hissing sound. These latter properties prove the myths of spiritual presence. The biblical burning bush that was not consumed may have been displaying one form of St. Elmo's Fire.[2]

30.2 Scientific explanation

Ball lightning is a natural phenomenon, or debatably, a pseudoscientific theory. It is sometimes associated with thunderstorms. It takes the form of a long-lived, glowing, floating object, as opposed to the short-lived arcing between two points commonly associated with lightning. An early attempt to explain ball lightning was recorded by Nikola Tesla on March 5, 1904.

There may, however, be special forms of plasma for which the above arguments do not fully apply. In particular, a plasma may be composed of negative and positive ions, rather than electrons and positive ions. In that case, the recombination may be rather slow even at ambient temperature. One such theory involves positively charged hydrogen and negatively charged nitrites (NO_2-) and nitrates (NO_3-). In that theory, the role of the ions as seeds for the condensation of water droplets plays an important role.

Ball lightning has also been seen to appear inside an aircraft, which has a metallic skin. Since the electric field cannot penetrate metal, there is a possibility ball lightning could be some form of induction phenomenon.

30.3 References

[1] "The Fire Of St. Elmo". Retrieved 2008-08-09.

[2] "The Fire Of St. Elmo". Retrieved 2008-08-09.

Chapter 31

Sarangay

Sarangay is a creature resembling a bull with a huge muscular body and a jewel attached to its ears.[1] It is the Philippine counterpart for the Greek minotaur. They are illustrated to be half bull and half man.

According to old folklore, *Sarangays* have a jewel or a precious gemstone in their ears that they are protecting. Those who try to steal it from them will be killed mercilessly. It was also said that when a *Sarangay* gets angry, its nose emits smoke.[2]

31.1 References

[1] "Da Adventure of Pendro Penduko". Retrieved 2008-10-09.

[2] *Mga Engkanto: A Bestiary of Filipino Fairies*. Philippines: eLf ideas Publication. 2003.

Chapter 32

Sarimanok

This article is about the mythical bird. For the boat, see Sarimanok (vinta).

The **Sarimanok** is a legendary bird of the Maranao people who originate from Mindanao, a major island in the Philippines. It comes from the words "sari" and "manok." *"Sari"* means cloth or garment, which is generally of assorted colors.[1] *Manòk* means "bird".

32.1 Description

It is the legendary bird that has become a ubiquitous symbol of Maranao art. It is depicted as a fowl with colorful wings and feathered tail, holding a fish on its beak or talons. The head is profusely decorated with scroll, leaf, and spiral motifs. It is said to be a symbol of good fortune.[2][3][4]

32.2 Origin

The Sarimanok is derived from a totem bird of the Maranao people, called *Itotoro*. According to the Maranao people, the *Itotoro* is a medium to the spirit world via its unseen twin spirit bird called *Inikadowa*.

The Sarimanok is also believed to have originated from the Garuda of Hindu epic Ramayana[5] adopted into Maharadia Lawana [6] of Maranao people, which in turn was later adopted to an Islamic legend after Southern Philippines converted to Islam.

According to the later Islamic legend, Muhammad found a rooster in the first of the seven heavens. The bird was so large its crest touched the second heaven. Its crow roused every living creature except man. Judgement day would come once this celestial rooster ceased to crow.[7]

A Maranao legend also says of a Sultan's daughter being swept by a colorful rooster that became a handsome young man and they were never seen ever again. The Sultan then created replicas of the bird to remember his daughter by.[8]

32.3 Cultural Significance

According to the tradition, the sarimanok is never displayed by itself. It must be displayed with the set of flags, standards and vexilloids. At present, this is not totally true; sarimanok may be placed on the top of the umbrella of a Sultan or dignitary, and also, the Mindanao State University has adopted it for the graduation exercises following a non-traditional use.[9][10]

Philippine National Artist Abdulmari Asia Imao uses the Sarimanok as a motif for some of his artworks which helped popularize the creature.[11]

The Far Eastern University seal bears the FEU Coat of Arms and the sarimanok motif. The FEU Coat of arms consists of eight-pointed golden star that represents the first eight main disciplines of FEU. The sarimanok is a legendary bird in full color that project the nationalistic spirit upon which the university is founded. The university wanted to have a Filipino touch in everything because they were one of the first universities in the Philippines to be founded by a pure-blooded Filipino, Dr. Nicanor Reyes, Sr..[12]

32.4 References

[1] "The Sarimanok". *The Pinoy Warrior*. Retrieved 12 August 2015.

[2] Philippine Arts and Culture: Sarimanok. Accessed August 28, 2008.

[3] Geocities: Sarimanok. Accessed August 28, 2008.

[4] Kipas: Kulintang Ensemble. Accessed August 28, 2008.

[5] http://theberntraveler.wordpress.com/2013/12/02/hudhud-and-darangen-voices-from-pre-colonial-philippines/

[6] https://openlibrary.org/books/OL3279931M/Maharadia_Lawana

[7] The Manila Times Internet Edition: Adorning the Sarimanok. Accessed July 29, 2007

[8] Philippine Culture: Sarimanok

[9] Royal Sultanates of Lake Lanao. Accessed August 28, 2008.

[10] ABC: Under the Crescent Moon. Accessed August 28, 2008.

[11] "Abdulmari Asia Imao". National Commission for Culture and the Arts. Retrieved 12 August 2015.

[12] Tambayan, The Official Magazine of the FEU Advocate, March 2012, Vol.8

32.5 External links

- Filipino Culture

Chapter 33

Sigbin

The **Sigbin** or **Sigben** is a creature in Philippine mythology said to come out at night to suck the blood of victims from their shadows. It is said to walk backwards with its head lowered between its hind legs, and to have the ability to become invisible to other creatures, especially humans. It resembles a hornless goat, but has very large ears which it can clap like a pair of hands and a long, flexible tail that can be used as a whip.It is said that their faeces is gold [1] The *Sigbin* is said to emit a nauseating odor.

It is believed to issue forth from its lair during Holy Week, looking for children that it will kill for their hearts, which it fashions into amulets.

According to legend, there are families known as *Sigbinan* ("those who own *Sigbin*") whose members possess the power to command these creatures, and are said to keep the *Sigbin* in jars made of clay. The *Aswang* are said to keep them as pets, along with another mythical creature, a bird known as the *Wak Wak*.[2]

There is speculation that the legend may be based on sightings of an actual animal species that is rarely seen; based on the description of the *Sigbin* in popular literature, the animal species might be related to the kangaroo.[2] With the recent discovery in the island of Borneo of the cat-fox,[3] a potential new species of carnivore described as having hind legs that are longer than its front legs, it has been postulated that reported sightings of *Sigbin* may actually be sightings of a member or relative of the cat-fox species.

The myth is popularly known in Visayas Islands and Mindanao.

33.1   In popular culture

The *Sigbin* is the object of song by the Visayan band Junior Kilat, entitled *Original Sigbin*.[4]

33.2   See also

- Peuchen

- Chupacabra

- Pedro Penduko

33.3   References

[1] Ramos, Maximo D. (1971). *Creatures of Philippine Lower Mythology*. Philippines: University of the Philippines Press.

[2] Tiempo, Edilberto K. "The Witch". Retrieved 2007-07-22.

[3] Meek, James (2005-12-07). "On the trail of the Borneo cat-fox". The Guardian. Retrieved 2007-07-23.

[4] "Original Sigbin". Retrieved 2007-07-22.

33.4 External Links

- Filipino Folklore: Sigbin

Chapter 34

Sirena (Philippine mythology)

The Sirens of Greek mythology are sometimes portrayed in later folklore as fully aquatic and mermaid-like; the fact that in Spanish, French, Italian, Polish, Romanian, Portuguese and Filipino the word for mermaid is respectively Sirena, Sirène, Sirena, Syrena, Sirenă, Sereia and **Sirena** and that in biology the Sirenia comprise an order of fully aquatic mammals that includes the dugong and manatee, add to the visual confusion, so that Sirens are even represented as mermaids. However, "the sirens, though they sing to mariners, are not sea-maidens," Harrison had cautioned; "they dwell on an island in a flowery meadow." In the Philippine mythology, the *Sirena* is a mythological aquatic creature with the head and torso of human female and the tail of a fish.[1] The male version of a *Sirena* is called a *Sireno*. Sometimes it is also paired with *Siyokoy* (see below). The *Sirena* is an *engkanto* which is classified as one of the *Bantay Tubig* or the guardians of water. In addition to the *Sirena*, other examples of *Bantay Tubig* are *Sireno*, *Siyokoy*, *Kataw* and *Ugkoy*. *Bantay Tubig* are part fish, part human water-dwelling *engkantos* which are the Filipino counterpart of the English merfolk.[2] A popular mermaid character in the Philippines is Dyesebel.

It is also said that the *Sirena* has a very beautiful and enchanting voice that can attract and hypnotize males, especially fishermen. A Sirena would sometimes sing to sailors and enchant them, distracting them from their work and causing them to walk off the deck or cause shipwrecks. They would sing with enchanting voices while hiding among the rocks by the shore. When the men hear their song they are hypnotized and the *Sirena* can abduct them. Some old folk traditions claim that the *Sirena* carry its victims under the sea and offer them to their water deities. Other stories claim that the *Sirena* squeezes the life out of drowning men while trying to rescue them.

A malevolent *Sirena* may tease and attract human males with their spellbinding songs; but reports of *Sirena* grabbing the seemingly hypnotized humans and drowning them or taking them under water may only be isolated cases. Either the tempted human had tried to chase the *Sirena* deep into the water until he drowned or he had a heart attack upon seeing such an *engkanto* and plunged literally into the water to his death.[3]

Dugongs, sea turtles, and small cetaceans such as dolphins usually accompany the *Sirena*.[4]

34.1 References

[1] Waterhouse, John William. "Mermaid". Retrieved 2008-08-09.

[2] *Mga Engkanto: A Bestiary of Filipino Fairies*. Philippines: eLf ideas Publication. 2003.

[3] *Mga Engkanto: A Bestiary of Filipino Fairies*. Philippines: eLf ideas Publication. 2003.

[4] *Mga Engkanto: A Bestiary of Filipino Fairies*. Philippines: eLf ideas Publication. 2003.

Chapter 35

Siyokoy (Philippine mythology)

The **Siyokoy** (**Syokoy**) are creatures in Philippine Mythology which were members of *Bantay Tubig* (merfolk). They are usually illustrated as green-skinned humanoids that have scaly body coverings, webbed hands and feet, having fins on several parts of their bodies.

35.1 Distinguishing characteristic

Compared to *Sirena*, *Sireno*, and *Kataw* who have human features, *Siyokoys* are of animalic in physical form and structure.[1] Some people describe *Siyokoy* as...

> ...horrifying sea creatures with fish-like bodies and long green tentacles. They drown mortals and eat them. They have gill slits, are colored brown or green, and have scaly skin, comparable to that of fishes.[2]

Intimidating aquatic animals such as eels, octopus, rays and squids usually swim along with *Siyokoy*.[1]

35.2 External Links

- Filipino Folklore Syokoy

35.3 References

[1] *Mga Engkanto: A Bestiary of Filipino Fairies*. Philippines: eLf ideas Publication. 2003.

[2] "Philippine mythical creatures". Retrieved 2008-09-13.

Chapter 36

Tagbanwa mythology

The **Tagbanwa mythology** is part of the religious beliefs and superstitions that has shaped the Tagbanwa way of life. It shares certain similarities with that of other ethnic groups in the Philippines, such as in the belief in heaven, hell and the human soul.

36.1 The Tagbanwa deities

36.1.1 Major gods

- **Mangindusa** or **Nagabacaban** - the highest-ranking deity who lives in *Awan-awan*, the region beyond the *Langit*; the god of the heavens; the punisher of crime;

- **Polo** - the benevolent god of the sea; whose help is invoked during the time of illness

- **Sedumunadoc** - the god of the earth, whose favor is sought in order to have a good harvest

- **Tabiacoud** the god of the underworld in the deep bowels of the earth

36.1.2 The Diwatas

The diwatas control the rain, and they are believed to be the creator of the world and of the human beings. They live where the tree trunks that hold up the *Langit* ("an infinitely high canopy"), which is the visible celestial region.

- **Diwata Kat Sidpan** - a deity who lives in *Sidpan* (West)

- **Diwata Kat Libatan** - a deity who lives in *Babatan* (East)

36.1.3 Celestial beings

- **Bugawasin** - the wife of Mangindusa

- **Tungkuyanin** - sits on the edge of *Langit*, with his feet dangling in the vastness of the cosmos and his eyes always cast down toward the earth

- **Tumangkuyun** - washes the trunks of the trees that hold up the *Langit* with blood of Tagbanwa who died in epidemics

- **Bulalakaw** or **Diwata Kat Dibuwat** - flying deities who roam the region of the clouds, ready to come to the aid of any Tagbanwa needing their help

36.1.4 Other deities

- **Taliyakad** - the watcher who guards the vine bridge called *Balugu*

- **Anggugru** - the "keeper of the fire," who welcomes the soul to the underworld and gives it fire

36.2 The Tagbanwa spirit world

- **Awan-Awan** - the zenith, or the area beyond *Langit*; the place where Mangindusa reigns from

- **Langit** - the visible celestial region where *Tungkuyanin* sits from

- **Sidpan** - the West; the placewhere *Diwata Kat Sidpan* lives at

- **Babatan** - the East; the place where *Diwata Kat Libatan* lives at

- **Dibuwat** - the skyworld of the *Bulalakaw* or *Diwata Kat Dibuwat* (flying deities); the "high" region; the place where souls who died of poisoning and violence roam around

- **Kiyabusan** - the place where souls who died of epidemics or sickness go to

- **Basad** - the underworld; the place where souls who died of natural death travels to

- **Material world** - refers to the environment; where souls who died of evil spirits or environmental causes inhabit

36.3 The Tagbanwa soul

A Tagbanwa is believed to have six souls in all. A "true soul" called *kiyarulwa*, and five secondary souls called the *payu*. The *kiyarulwa* is a gift of Mangindusa to a child emerging from the mother's womb, while the other souls appear only during the *lambay* ritual for the child upon reaching one month or two. *Lambay* is any ceremony, which is directly addressed to Mangindusa. These other souls are found at the extremities of the hands and feet, and on top of the head. When a person dies the *kiyarulwa* wanders to four possible destinations. If the cause of death is epidemic or sickness, then the soul will go to the *Kiyabusan*, they become known as the *salakap*. If a person from poisoning or violence the souls goes to inhabit the *Dibuwat*. Those who died because their souls were caught by the environmental or evil spirits - their soul will transform into *biyaladbad* and will inhabit the environment. If a person dies of natural death, the souls travels to *Basad*, the underworld, and becomes the *tiladmanin*.

When a Tagbanwa dies, his or her soul remains on earth for seven days, until the *kapupusan* or rites for the dead are finished. For seven days, the soul lingers on in the grave at daytime, but returns to its former house at night to observe the behavior of those left behind.

36.3.1 Basad

In the its journey to the underworld, the soul encounters several places. These include:

- **Kalabagang** - the sacred river where souls meets *Taliyakad*

- **Balugu** - the vine bridge

In *Basad*, the spirits of the dead live a life that mirrors exactly that of the living. But everything is the reverse of what happens in the world of living. As the sun rises on earth, it goes down in *Basad* or planting time on earth is harvest time in *Basad*.

36.4   The Tagbanwa rituals

36.4.1   Lambay

The *lambay* is held two times a year. It is observed first in January, and involves ritual appears to the deities for days of sunshine and winds that sufficiently dry the forests and prepare them for clearing and planting. A second one is held in May, when the people ask for moderate rains that will make their upland rice grows.

There are two rituals, which seeks protection for all Tagbanwa wherever they may be, from the feared *salakap*, the spirits of epidemic, sickness and death. These two rituals are the *pagbuyis* and the *runsay*.

36.4.2   Pagbuyis

The *pagbuyis* is performed three times a year. The first is in November, and second in December. The third is when the moon can be seen during the daytime, called *magkaaldawan*.

36.4.3   Runsay

The *runsay* is described as the most dramatic of all Tagbanwa rituals. It is observed only once a year, at nighttime, on the fourth day after the full moon of December. It takes place on the beach near the mouth of the Aborlan River. The *runsay*, like the *pagbuyis*, is held to ask for protection against epidemic. The ritual begins at dusk and ends at dawn.

Phases of Runsay

There are five distinct phases in the *runsay*. These include:

- 1st phase - the building of the *bangkaran* or banglay, a 3.6m ceremonial raft

- 2nd phase - the *panawag*, invocation to the spirits of the dead and the nine deities who rode the kawa on the sea; the burning of incense on the *kadiyang* atop the *bangkaran*; prayers by the rituals leader; lighting of the candle and offering of ritual foods to the deities

- 3rd phase - the second call to the deities to partake of the food, which the signal for the children to dive into the mound of food on the raft, and eat as much as they can; and the cleaning up and repair of the raft.

- 4th phase - the third invocation to the nine deities, followed by the individual family offerings represented by a woman; the tying of the chicken to the platform and the lighting of candles beside it; the hoisting of the raft towards the sea; the re-lighting of candles blown out by the wind; the throwing of a pinch of rice to the sea; and the voyage seaward of the bankaran.

- 5th phase - includes group singing and dancing after the raft has disappeared

36.4.4   Pagdiwata

At the center of the *diwata* rituals is the babaylan, who has the responsibility of selecting the areas for a new clearing, placating the spirits of the surroundings, providing magical charms for hunters and fishers, and curing all kinds of ailments. While any adult can invoke the spirits of the dead in other Tagbanwa rituals, only the babaylan can summon them in the *pagdiwata*.

36.4.5 Bilang

The *bilang* ceremony is the all-important ritual for the dead. It takes place after the rice harvest, a time when *tabad* becomes plentiful. Every family is expected to host one or more *bilang* rituals. The *bilang* rituals begin with the rite of divination, to determine which among the spirit relatives has caused a person's illness. This makes use of the babaylan, who performs the brief rite of *panawag* near the grave of the dead relative by making offerings of the betel quids and ceremonial cigarettes, and promises *tabad* should the ill become well. The celebrants together with the offerings prepare a jar of *tabad* with sipping reeds. The *bilang* ceremony involves the *paurut* (invocation) of as many spirit relatives as possible through incantation, and the burning of the *parina* (incense) whose pleasant smells attract the deities and spirits of the dead. The gongs are played as the *paurut* is being performed, and their music is an added incentive for the spirit to descend on the gathering. After the ritual offering of the articles have been laid out on the mat, the food is distributed to the children first, and then to the guests; then the *bilang* mat is removed. The communal drinking of *tabad* through the reed straws follows, a very festive social event that lasts through the night.[1]

36.5 References

[1] Tagabanua by Mark Joel Velasquez. Accessed August 28, 2008.

Chapter 37

Tikbalang

Tikbalang (also written as **Tigbalang**, **Tigbalan**, or **Tikbalan**) is a creature of Philippine folklore said to lurk in the mountains and forests of the Philippines. It is generally described as a tall, bony humanoid creature with disproportionately long limbs, to the point that its knees reach above its head when it squats down.[1] It has the head and feet of an animal, most commonly a horse. It is sometimes believed to be a transformation of an aborted fetus which has been sent to earth from limbo.[2]

37.1 Superstitions

Tikbalangs are said to scare travelers and lead them astray. Tikbalangs play tricks on travelers such that they keep on returning to an arbitrary path no matter how far he goes or where he turns. Supposedly this is counteracted by wearing one's shirt inside out. Another countermeasure is to ask permission out loud to pass by or, not to produce too much noise while in the woods in order not to offend or disturb the tikbalang.

A superstition popular with the Tagalog of Rizal Province is that Tikbalangs are benevolent guardians of elemental kingdoms. They are usually found standing at the foot of large trees looking around for anyone who dare to bestow malignancy on their kingdom's territory.

A common saying has it that rain from a clear sky means "*may kinakasal na tikbalang.*"(Filipino, "a tikbalang is getting married".) This was potentially connected with a similar Spanish proverb that claimed a witch was getting married when there was rain on a sunny day, although many cultures have such sayings in which a trickster figure gets married (cp. fox's wedding, bear's wedding, monkey's birthday).

According to traditional folklore, the tikbalang can also transform itself into human form or turn invisible to humans. They like to lead travelers astray.[1]

Tikbalang are generally associated with dark, sparsely populated, foliage-overgrown areas, with legends variously identifying their abode as being beneath bridges, in Bamboo or Banana groves, and atop Kalumpang (Sterculia foetida)[3] or Balite (Ficus indica) trees.

37.2 Taming a tikbalang

By one account a tikbalang has a mane of sharp spines, with the three thickest of these being of particular importance. A person who obtains one of these spines can use them as an *anting-anting* (talisman) in order to keep the tikbalang as his servant. The tikbalang must first be subdued, however, by leaping onto it and tying it with a specially-prepared cord. The would-be-tamer must then hang on while the creature flies through the air, fighting madly to dislodge its unwelcome rider, until it is exhausted and acknowledges its defeat.[2] or you can look on his mane and you will see 3 golden hairs and if you pluck 3 of them before he/she eats you, they will serve you until you die.

37.3   In popular culture

37.3.1   Literature

- Within the Lemegeton the 55th goetic spirit Orobas has the physical appearance of a tikbalang.

- A tikbalang named Lusyo features prominently in The Mythology Class, a graphic novel written and illustrated by Filipino comic creator Arnold Arre.[4]

- X-Men and Wetworks illustrator Whilce Portacio has created a comic book series called Stone: The Awakening, which features Filipino legendary creatures, including the tikbalang.

- A tale including a tikbalang appears in *When the Elephants Dance* by Tess Uriza Holthe. The wise creature mentors a young Filipino man who can see ghosts that haven't yet passed on.

- A tikbalang is the antagonist of the issue "Rules of the Race" in the comic *Trese*, where it engages in street races with unwitting drivers.[5]

- *Tikbalang Kung Kabilugan ng Buwan* is a child-friendly telling of the Tikbalang mythos – written by Victoria Añonuevo, illustrated by Kora Dandan-Albano and released by Adarna House – intended to familiarize young Filipino audiences with Philippine Mythological creatures. In the story, a Tikbalang becomes lonely for lack of a playmate during the full moon, a time when Filipino children of generations past traditionally went out to play in the moonlight. In search for a playmate, the Tikbalang leaves his home in the Kalumpang tree and encounters first a Kapre, then a Nuno, an Aswang, and a Tiyanak, before he finally meets another Tikbalang as a suitable playmate.[3]

37.3.2   Film

- The 2008 animated film Dayo: Sa Mundo ng Elementalia features the Tikbalang as one of the main creatures of the story.

- A Tikbalang like creature was featured in the 2002 film Spirit Warriors: The Shortcut, where it is descrbed as brown hairy gigantic creature which is similar to the height of a Kapre, where it helps Red and Thor escape while they were attaked by a group of Aswangs.

- *Tikbalang: The Horse Demon* was the first episode of the 2015 Creatures Of Philippine Mythology documentary web-series produced by The Aswang Project and High Banks Entertainment Ltd. It traces back the origin of the Tikbalang's image to India, circa 2000BCE, and follows its evolution to modern day.[6]

37.3.3   Television

- The 2010 television show Lost Girl has a Tikbalang as a one time foe. Its appearance differs from the one that is in the Philippine Mythology, which is described as a humanoid grass like creature which is similar of that Man-Thing.

- ABS-CBN 2013 television series Juan dela Cruz leading the Tikbalang and Enkanto as Juan's allies against Peruha and the Aswang legions.

37.3.4   Music

- The Filipino hardcore band, Tame the Tikbalang is named after this creature, and the common motif of "taming" one.

37.3.5   Video games

- The popular MMORPG World of Warcraft features a character named "Griftah" who sells an amulet called an "Infallible Tikbalang Ward". The accompanying text states, "With this trusty warding talisman, no tikbalang will ever find you and steal you away to the treetops. It really works!" When an item in World of Warcraft is said to "really work", it seldom does; naturally, tikbalangs are not found in the game.

- In the MMORPG Final Fantasy XI, Tikbalang is a rare monster belonging to the Tauri family (demonic humanoids composed of various animal parts, capable of inflicting a lethal curse if you do not avert your eyes.)

- Tikbalang also appears in MMORPG Ragnarok Online as a giant armored horse in Malaya Port, a city based in Philippines.

37.4   See also

- Sihuanaba

- Other Filipino mythological creatures

37.5   References

- Blair, Emma Helen; Edward Gaylord Bourne, James Alexander Robertson, John Boyd Thacher (1905). *The Philippine Islands, 1493–1803*. The A. H. Clark company. pp. 269–270. ASIN B000858BO4.[7]

- Bergaño, Diego (1860). *Vocabulario de la lengua Pampangan en romance* (in Spanish). Ramirez y Giruadier. p. 254.[8]

37.6   Additional reading

- Cruz, Neal (31 October 2008). "As I See It:Philippine mythological monsters". *Philippine Daily Inquirer*.

37.7   Footnotes

[1] Eugenio, Damiana L. (2008). *Philippine Folk Literature An Anthology*. University of the Philippines Press. p. 247. ISBN 978-971-542-536-0. Retrieved 2009-05-08.

[2] de los Reyes, Isabelo (1890). *El Folk-Lore Filipino* (in Spanish). Imprenta de Santa Cruz. pp. 66–69. ISBN 978-971-542-038-9.

[3] Añouevo, Victoria; Dandan-Albano, Kora (2004). *Ang Tikbalang Kung Kabilugan ng Buwan*. Quezon City: Adarna House, Inc. ISBN 978-971-508-250-1.

[4] Lourd de Veyra (4th Quarter, 1999). "Gen X Meets Tikbalang". FLY Magazine. Retrieved 2006-01-12. Check date values in: |date= (help)

[5] Tan, Budjette. "Case 2: Rules of the Race." *Trese: Murder on Balete Drive*. Illust. Kajo Baldisimo. Pasay City: Visual Print, 2008.

[6] Clark, Jordan "Tikbalang: The Horse Demon" Episode 01, *Creatures Of Philippine Mythology* (2015) https://www.youtube.com/watch?v=gRUSBSJ39KY

[7] *the philippine islands 1493–1898*. 1905. p. 269.

[8] *Vocabulario de la lengua pampanga*. 1860.

37.8 External links

- Keith Thompson's rendition of a tikbalang.

Chapter 38

Tiyanak

The **Tiyanak** (also **Tianak** or **Tianac**[1]) is a vampiric creature in Philippine mythology that imitates the form of a child. It usually takes the form of a newborn baby and cries like one in the jungle to attract unwary travelers. Once it is picked up by the victim, it reverts to its true form and attacks the victim.[2] The tiyanak is also depicted to take malevolent delight in leading travelers astray,[3] or in abducting children.[4]

38.1 Appearance and characteristics

While various legends have slightly different versions of the tiyanak folklore, the stories all agree on its ability to mimic an infant, with its ability to imitate an infant's cries for luring victims.[3] In some legends, the Tiyanak may take the form of a specific child.[5]

- In one version, it retains the general shape of a baby but then forms sharp claws and fangs to attack its victim.[2]

- In another, it shares certain similarities with dwarfs and is similarly associated with the earth. In this version, the "true" form of the tiyanak is that of a little old man with wrinkled skin, a long beard and mustache, a flat nose and eyes the size of peseta coins. The same story says that a tiyanak is relatively immobile because its right leg is much shorter than the other. This deformity forces it to move by leaping rather than walking, making it difficult to hunt or stalk victims, but its ability to mimic an infant's cry compensates for this disadvantage.[3]

- In yet another story it is seen supernaturally flying through the forest (still in the form of a baby)[6] and in a legend from the island of Mindoro it transforms into a black bird before flying away[5]

- In another version from Pampanga, the tiyanak are described as small, nut-brown people who don't walk on the ground but rather float on air. They have large noses, wide mouths, large fierce eyes and sharp voices.[4]

38.2 Origins

There are various stories on how tiyanaks came to being. The Mandaya people of Mindanao claim that the tiyanak is the spirit of a child whose mother died before giving birth. This caused it to be "born in the ground", thus gaining its current state.[3] A similar supernatural creature in Malay folklore is the Pontianak, which was a woman who died before giving birth.

With the Spanish colonization of the Philippines in the 16th century, the tiyanak myth was integrated into Christianity. The tiyanak in the Christian version were supposedly the souls of infants that died before being baptized. In modern-day Philippines, this definition has extended to that of aborted fetuses that returned from death to seek revenge on those who deprived them of life.[2]

38.3 Countermeasures

In local belief, various countermeasures are supposedly effective against the tiyanak. Those that were led astray by the creature's cries are believed to be able to break the enchantment by turning their clothes inside out. The tiyanak finds the method humorous enough to let go of the traveler and go back to the jungles. Loud noises such as a New Year's celebration are also thought to be enough to drive the tiyanak away from the vicinity.[3] Objects believed to repel Aswang (vampiric shape-shifters), like garlic and the rosary, are also commonly believed to be effective against the tiyanak.[2]

38.4 In popular culture

The tiyanak is the subject of many Philippine movies:

- *Tianak* (1953)[7]

- *Tiyanak* (1988)[8]

- *Juan Tanga, super naman, at ang kambal na tiyanak* (1990)[9]

- *Impakto* (1996)

- *Tiyanaks* (2007)[10]

Tiyanaks appear in week-32 2013 episodes of Juan dela Cruz (TV series).

The Tiyanak is also featured as a monster, along with other Philippine folklore-inspired beings, in the Port Malaya patch of Ragnarok Online.[11]

38.5 External Links

- Filipino Folklore:Tiyanak

38.6 See also

- Toyol

38.7 References

[1] Damiana L, Eugenio (2007). *Philippine Folk Literature: An Anthology Volume 1 of Philippine Folk Literature Series.* UP Press. p. 249. ISBN 9715425364.

[2] Paraiso, Salvador; Jose Juan Paraiso (2003). *The Balete Book: A collection of demons, monsters and dwarfs from the Philippine lower mythology.* Philippines: Giraffe Books. ISBN 971-8832-79-3.

[3] Ramos, Maximo D. (1971). *Creatures of Philippine Lower Mythology.* Philippines: University of the Philippines Press.

[4] Eugenio, Damiana (2002). *Philippine Folk Literature: The Legends.* Quezon City: University of the Philippines Press. p. 490. ISBN 971-542-357-4.

[5] Adelina Del Rosario (1975). "Isang Pag-aaral ng mga kuwentong bayan ng Oriental Mindoro". University of the Philippines.

[6] Gardner, Fletcher (1906). "Philippine (Tagalog) Superstitions". *Superstitions Journal of American Folklore* (The Journal of American Folklore, Vol. 19, No. 74) **19** (April–June): 191–204. doi:10.2307/534566. JSTOR 534566.

[7] *Tianak* at the Internet Movie Database

[8] *Tiyanak* at the Internet Movie Database

[9] *Juan Tanga, super naman, at ang kambal na tiyanak* at the Internet Movie Database

[10] *Tiyanaks* at the Internet Movie Database

[11] Otakultura.com (2011). "Malaya Map Revealed!". Retrieved on 2011-09-01.

38.8   Additional reading

- Cruz, Neal (2008-10-31). "As I See It:Philippine mythological monsters". *Philippine Daily Inquirer*.

Chapter 39

Wakwak

The **Wakwak** is a vampiric, bird-like creature in Philippine mythology. It is said to snatch humans at night as prey, similar to the *Manananggal* and the *Ekek* in rural areas of the Philippines, due to its ability to fly. The difference between the *Mananggal* and the *Wakwak* is that *Wakwak* cannot separate its torso from its body while the *Manananggal* can. Some believe it is also a form a vampire takes. Other people contend that a "Wakwak" is a Philippine night bird belonging to a witch.

The sound of a *Wakwak* is usually associated with the presence of an *Unglu* (vampire) or *Ungo* (ghost or monster). It is also believed that this monster is called "Wakwak" due to this sound it makes when it flaps its wings while flying. When one hears the *Wakwak*, it is looking for possible victims. If the sound of the *Wakwak* is loud, it means it is far from you. Otherwise, it is near and worse yet, it is about to attack. It slashes and mutilates its victims and feeds on their hearts.

The *Wakwak* is often described by old folks to have long sharp talons and a pair of wings similar to those of a bat. It uses its talons or claws to slash its victims and to get their heart. Many say that its wings are also sharp as a knife.[1]

The sound that a *tiki*, *tike* or *teke* (common house gecko) makes usually at night when out of sight was discovered by an American who spent much time in the Philippines to be the source of the sound everyone was saying was a "Wakwak".

"A Dictionary of Cebuano Visaya" by John U. Wolff published by Cornell University, South East Asia Program and Linguistic Society of the Philippines 1972 defines Wak Wak as:

1. wakwak$_1$

    noun bird which comes out at night, so called from its call. Its call signifies the presence of a vampire (unglo) or in some beliefs. it is a form the vampire takes himself.

    verb 1 [A13] for the wakwak to be about; 2 [a12] victimize someone with vampiritic activity. paN-*verb* [A2] go about engaging in vampiritic activity. -un *noun* = UNGLU, *noun*

2. wakwak$_2$ *noun* the West piece of Mahjong = WISTL.

Also **Wak-Wak** in early Philippine history was the Kingdom of Wak-Wak along with the Kingdom of Zabag and were situated in Pampanga[2]

39.1   See also

- Peuchen

- Sigbin

39.2   References

[1] *Mga Engkanto: A Bestiary of Filipino Fairies.* Philippines: eLf ideas Publication. 2003.

[2] The Medieval Geography of Sanfotsi and Zabag

39.3   External links

- Filipino Folklore:Wakwak

39.4 Text and image sources, contributors, and licenses

39.4.1 Text

- **Agta (mythical creature)** *Source:* https://en.wikipedia.org/wiki/Agta_(mythical_creature)?oldid=669162920 *Contributors:* Rpyle731, Cesium 133, Truthanado, Yobot, AnomieBOT, GoingBatty, Miszatomic, TheJJJunk, Sourov0000 and Nanayangel

- **Alan (legendary creature)** *Source:* https://en.wikipedia.org/wiki/Alan_(legendary_creature)?oldid=616938287 *Contributors:* Theinfo, JuJube, OrangeDog, The Rogue Penguin, Rodsan18, Cydebot, Kotengu, Goldenrowley, Lenticel, CommonsDelinker, Wowowee 13, ImageRemovalBot, ClueBot, Axxand, Tsange, Vinniemon, Citation bot, ReddFighter, FrescoBot, PigFlu Oink, Alan.poindexter, RioHondo and Anonymous: 15

- **Amalanhig** *Source:* https://en.wikipedia.org/wiki/Amalanhig?oldid=659862650 *Contributors:* Rjwilmsi, Cydebot, JaGa, Ian.thomson, CultureDrone, ImageRemovalBot, Vinniemon, DASHBot, Arestheg0d444 and Anonymous: 1

- **Amomongo** *Source:* https://en.wikipedia.org/wiki/Amomongo?oldid=671030867 *Contributors:* Rich Farmbrough, TexasAndroid, CambridgeBayWeather, Apokryltaros, GiantSnowman, Cydebot, Ameliorate!, Kguirnela, VolkovBot, ImageRemovalBot, Otolemur crassicaudatus, Addbot, FarmerDavid, TaBOT-zerem, Vinniemon, RedBot, H3llBot, RioHondo, NightXenon999 and Anonymous: 5

- **Anggitay** *Source:* https://en.wikipedia.org/wiki/Anggitay?oldid=684165381 *Contributors:* Asarelah, Cydebot, ImageRemovalBot, Axxand, Addbot, Luckas-bot, AnakngAraw, Vinniemon, DrilBot, DASHBot and Anonymous: 5

- **Aswang** *Source:* https://en.wikipedia.org/wiki/Aswang?oldid=688450343 *Contributors:* Seav, Ronz, Emperor, Maximus Rex, Dimadick, Fredrik, Jondel, Davidcannon, DocWatson42, Lucky 6.9, Suhit Kelkar, Kaldari, PFHLai, Sam Hocevar, Histrion, Bluemask, Mike Rosoft, Discospinster, Rich Farmbrough, Xxlitleonexx, LoganCale, Antaeus Feldspar, RoyBoy, Stesmo, Kundor, Alansohn, V2Blast, Wtmitchell, Firsfron, Woohookitty, Flyinghamster39, Sjö, Rjwilmsi, Jason.cinema, YurikBot, Gaius Cornelius, CambridgeBayWeather, Taed, Dogcow, BOT-Superzerocool, Elf ideas, Croat Canuck, Bentong Isles, ArielGold, SmackBot, MattieTK, Ema Zee, Gilliam, Richfife, Keegan, MalafayaBot, The Rogue Penguin, MyNameIsVlad, Chicbicyclist, WayKurat, Khazar, Rodsan18, Mgiganteus1, Udibi, JohnCD, Cydebot, Gogo Dodo, Beached Oil Tanker, VZG, 23prootie, N5iln, Vertium, Missvain, Woody, Indrek, Qwerty Binary, Hotridge, Askari Mark, Alternativity, Johnbrillantes, EagleFan, Mikangra, Lenticel, BAYANI98, CommonsDelinker, Jon2777, KylieTastic, STBotD, Davecrosby uk, VolkovBot, Cronosmantas, Bovineboy2008, TXiKiBoT, AlleborgoBot, Tiddly Tom, Exert, Dasmarinas71, Florentino floro, ImageRemovalBot, ClueBot, PipepBot, Boneyard90, Axxand, Bleubeatle, XLinkBot, Addbot, Lost on Belmont, Tassedethe, Teles, Yobot, Fraggle81, Gongshow, AnakngAraw, Viking59, IronLotus, Tsinitoboy, Magog the Ogre, AnomieBOT, Ineverremembermyaccount, Jim1138, Stoodtalk, Vinniemorano, Vinniemon, Materialscientist, Cyfraw, MLauba, Jztan, FrescoBot, Rock4, Moloch09, Citation bot 1, Jcnewfields, Sumone10154, Diannaa, Barghest23, Alagos, Zollerriia, GoingBatty, Solarra, TeleComNasSprVen, Shamankam, Donner60, Espiritufire, ClueBot NG, Kcevora85, Snotbot, CryptidTruth, Widr, Helpful Pixie Bot, BG19bot, Kai Ojima, Tess600, Darealchupacabra, Jonarge, Takayama812, Megamanxs, Faenonymous, EricEnfermero, Cerbera LM, Wes389, Kurtinzgroups, Epicgenius, Kap 7, SJ Defender, Anti-Racim 4556, Lors aspacio22, Marelia Mags Murari, Ca2james, Wmtbaker, Roalfb, Izrfernando, Autobrats, NerfersUnited, Contour777, Espenaching, SummerPhDv2.0, Kua mel and Anonymous: 251

- **Bakunawa** *Source:* https://en.wikipedia.org/wiki/Bakunawa?oldid=683624131 *Contributors:* Discospinster, Rich Farmbrough, Grenavitar, BD2412, NawlinWiki, Thiseye, Malcolma, Zvika, SmackBot, Elonka, The Rogue Penguin, Rodsan18, The Man in Question, Cydebot, 23prootie, Benstown, Alternativity, Johnbrillantes, Lenticel, CommonsDelinker, IBakunawai, ABF, SieBot, ImageRemovalBot, Lantan2004, Addbot, SwisterTwister, LilHelpa, Christopher610, MrX, Minimac, Wackyjabber, Khazar2, Rakista112, Kalbopoako and Anonymous: 30

- **Bal-Bal** *Source:* https://en.wikipedia.org/wiki/Bal-Bal?oldid=666177396 *Contributors:* Rjwilmsi, Vmenkov, Drdisque, Cydebot, ImageRemovalBot, Vinniemon, PigFlu Oink, DASHBot, Charmaster4 and Anonymous: 2

- **Balete Drive** *Source:* https://en.wikipedia.org/wiki/Balete_Drive?oldid=680842713 *Contributors:* Auric, Grutness, Josh Parris, Jaxhere, Nanami Kamimura, Luk, Hmains, Red marquis, Kittybrewster, Howard the Duck, WayKurat, Simply south, Phatom87, Cydebot, Fluxbot, DarkAudit, LuckyLouie, Kamuixtv, JL99, Swpb, The Kinslayer, STBot, Mines32, Pdcook, Cyberpaul~enwiki, Briarfallen, XLinkBot, Tassedethe, Lightbot, Boweneer, John of Reading, BG19bot, George Ponderevo, Laodah, Kj plma, RioHondo, Clarence froggy, Mogism, PhilippineRevolution and Anonymous: 21

- **Batibat** *Source:* https://en.wikipedia.org/wiki/Batibat?oldid=656814626 *Contributors:* President Rhapsody, Asarelah, The Rogue Penguin, Rodsan18, Cydebot, Synergy, Lenticel, Joemaza, Geekdiva, ImageRemovalBot, Vinniemon, Σ and Anonymous: 4

- **Berbalang (legendary creature)** *Source:* https://en.wikipedia.org/wiki/Berbalang_(legendary_creature)?oldid=616964627 *Contributors:* Rich Farmbrough, RJFJR, Woohookitty, Unforgiven24, Ergative rlt, Cydebot, Trey314159, R'n'B, Nono64, Fratrep, Auntof6, Addbot, AnakngAraw, Plaidbus, Kibi78704, Brickmack and Anonymous: 4

- **Berberoka** *Source:* https://en.wikipedia.org/wiki/Berberoka?oldid=684165676 *Contributors:* Rjwilmsi, RussBot, Asarelah, E Wing, Cydebot, ImageRemovalBot, Vinniemon and Anonymous: 4

- **Bungisngis** *Source:* https://en.wikipedia.org/wiki/Bungisngis?oldid=603748405 *Contributors:* Jondel, BD2412, Closedmouth, SmackBot, Cydebot, MarritzN, Lenticel, ImageRemovalBot, Axxand, Vinniemon, Hoverdrive, H3llBot, Majimbulok, Helpful Pixie Bot, Periglio, WOLF AS WHITE, Monkbot and Anonymous: 3

- **Busaw** *Source:* https://en.wikipedia.org/wiki/Busaw?oldid=630952303 *Contributors:* Rjwilmsi, Asarelah, John, Cydebot, Philg88, Tgeairn, Ian.thomson, ImageRemovalBot, Arjayay, Vinniemon, ClueBot NG, WOLF AS WHITE and Anonymous: 2

- **Dalaketnon** *Source:* https://en.wikipedia.org/wiki/Dalaketnon?oldid=634920391 *Contributors:* TheMolecularMan, Rjwilmsi, Cydebot, CultureDrone, ImageRemovalBot, Vinniemon, LilHelpa, DrilBot and Anonymous: 1

- **Diwata** *Source:* https://en.wikipedia.org/wiki/Diwata?oldid=682528812 *Contributors:* Seav, Jondel, Cobaltbluetony, Jojit fb, Kundor, OwenX, Tabletop, Ketiltrout, Pigman, EntChickie, Asarelah, Elf ideas, SmackBot, Mirokado, Bluebot, The Rogue Penguin, Phantomdadog, WayKurat, Rodsan18, Midnightblueowl, Joseph Solis in Australia, CmdrObot, Cydebot, 23prootie, Richard Relucio, Marek69, Cloudhand, Alternativity, Silentaria, Gunkarta, Coldmachine, ImageRemovalBot, SchreiberBike, XLinkBot, Lynyrdjym, Addbot, Lightbot, Yobot, Putol,

AnomieBOT, Byeitical, LilHelpa, Joaquin008, Hariboneagle927, Kibi78704, Ravishas3, Lukabaliw, ClueBot NG, GabrielPelareja, Jigzmoto, Jonarge, Randykamradt, Pansitkanton, Mogism, Masterpeace3, Theparties, Vansockslayer and Anonymous: 47

- **Ekek** *Source:* https://en.wikipedia.org/wiki/Ekek?oldid=684165296 *Contributors:* Ronz, BD2412, Rjwilmsi, TexasAndroid, Asarelah, Cydebot, ImageRemovalBot, Mr. Granger, Againme, Vinniemon, Joaquin008, Briankenpogi and Anonymous: 5

- **Engkanto** *Source:* https://en.wikipedia.org/wiki/Engkanto?oldid=629063739 *Contributors:* Circeus, BD2412, Rjwilmsi, Ecoleetage, BorgQueen, GiantSnowman, Cydebot, Eastmain, Julia Rossi, Sigurd Dragon Slayer, PhilKnight, Lenticel, Joshua Issac, Dpmuk, Zaharous, Fastily, Colibri37, Gail, L2ipp3l2, Yobot, Jim1138, Citation bot, Citation bot 1, DatuRajah II, ClueBot NG, CitationCleanerBot, Riley Huntley, LeFapOnymous, Epicgenius and Anonymous: 11

- **Kapre** *Source:* https://en.wikipedia.org/wiki/Kapre?oldid=686482833 *Contributors:* Ronz, Jondel, Benc, DocWatson42, DO'Neil, PFHLai, Mysidia, Ogress, Alansohn, DreamGuy, Shimeru, Tslocum, Bgwhite, Gooberliberation, Closedmouth, That Guy, From That Show!, SmackBot, The Rogue Penguin, Can't sleep, clown will eat me, Шизомби, Rodsan18, Kazansky, ShelfSkewed, Cydebot, Fayenatic london, Barek, Alternativity, Johnbrillantes, ClovisPt, Lenticel, Kguirnela, J.delanoy, LordAnubisBOT, Idioma-bot, TJ Elliot Scott, Humboldt, Dinoarbi, Tradereddy, Phynicen, Addbot, Kurtzilla, Materialscientist, DSisyphBot, FrescoBot, Lawlol123, Reconsider the static, PhiloBoy, Kylekrebs, EmausBot, ZéroBot, BenetVerzosa, ClueBot NG, BG19bot, PhnomPencil, Megamanxs, Haminoon, Piepatel3.14, Lors aspacio22, Mediavalia, Boompanesanghininga and Anonymous: 45

- **Kataw (Philippine mythology)** *Source:* https://en.wikipedia.org/wiki/Kataw_(Philippine_mythology)?oldid=341462103 *Contributors:* Cydebot, ImageRemovalBot, Axxand, Vinniemon and Anonymous: 3

- **Kumakatok** *Source:* https://en.wikipedia.org/wiki/Kumakatok?oldid=608578025 *Contributors:* Lockley, Zotel, SmackBot, Rodsan18, Cydebot, 23prootie, Nick Number, Lenticel, Ridernyc, Goustien, ClueBot NG, Monkbot and Anonymous: 5

- **Manananggal** *Source:* https://en.wikipedia.org/wiki/Manananggal?oldid=687328473 *Contributors:* Earth, Ronz, Christopher Sundita, Yosri, Jondel, Mushroom, DocWatson42, Evahala, PFHLai, Histrion, 96T, Kundor, OGoncho, Alansohn, JRHorse, Daduzi, Rtkat3, Wisekwai, Anomalocaris, Friday, Asarelah, Entheta, SmackBot, Master Deusoma, Chris the speller, The Rogue Penguin, Dlohcierekim's sock, Mrwuggs, OrphanBot, VMS Mosaic, Unknown Dragon, Caniago, Chicbicyclist, Bml, Kalathalan, J.smith, Rodsan18, Zero sharp, Tawkerbot2, Koshii, DangerousPanda, JohnCD, Iokseng, Andrea75, Cydebot, QuestionMark, Casliber, Smeazel, 23prootie, N5iln, Marek69, Thisisina, Kobe-WanKenobi, Scottandrewhutchins, Goldenrowley, Qwerty Binary, Leuko, Steelorange, Askari Mark, Alternativity, InternationalHit2, Lenticel, Nopira, Octopug, Joemaza, Kguirnela, Steelwater~enwiki, AntiSpamBot, Egard89, Vmaldia, Creationlog, Teredenz, BHenry1969, Jan1nad, Pokemon Buffy Titan, Boneyard90, Sisiluncai, Axxand, SchreiberBike, XLinkBot, Addbot, Yobot, Ptbotgourou, AnomieBOT, Ineverremembermyaccount, Jim1138, Vinniemorano, Mintrick, Materialscientist, The High Fin Sperm Whale, Leon3289, Kevyo, FrescoBot, Citation bot 1, Kibi78704, Alagos, Winner 42, ClueBot NG, Mtking, Girthgirl101, CeraBot, Capizboy, Teammm, Mogism, Cerbera LM, Kurtinzgroups, Itc editor2, FrB.TG, Ciaraleone, Monkbot, Poupapi, Phylsantos, GeniusA4tech and Anonymous: 112

- **Manaul** *Source:* https://en.wikipedia.org/wiki/Manaul?oldid=620189448 *Contributors:* ZayZayEM, TexasAndroid, GiantSnowman, Cydebot, Kguirnela, RedBot, EmausBot and Anonymous: 4

- **Mangindusa** *Source:* https://en.wikipedia.org/wiki/Mangindusa?oldid=558076308 *Contributors:* Wisdom89, Bazonka, Switchercat, Cydebot, Richard Relucio, T@nn, Goustien, Axxand, Reidlophile and DrilBot

- **Minokawa** *Source:* https://en.wikipedia.org/wiki/Minokawa?oldid=677884743 *Contributors:* Woohookitty, Rjwilmsi, Risssa, Cydebot, Maias, ImageRemovalBot, Meteorit~enwiki, Axxand, Lantan2004, Queenmomcat, AnomieBOT, Cueballer2690, Vinniemon, DrilBot, Updatehelper, EmausBot, ZéroBot and Anonymous: 3

- **Nuno** *Source:* https://en.wikipedia.org/wiki/Nuno?oldid=659603374 *Contributors:* Jondel, Marpeck, Gtrmp, SWAdair, Lucky 6.9, Oneiros, Ta bu shi da yu, Hydrox, Jojit fb, Jonathunder, Alansohn, Noit, FreplySpang, Dialectric, Nlu, Crisco 1492, HeleneSylvie, SmackBot, Canthusus, Francisco Valverde, Pfhreak, The Rogue Penguin, Tamfang, OrphanBot, Deiz, Rodsan18, Astuishin, Xiaphias, P199, Nehrams2020, JoeBot, Mujinga, Harej bot, Cydebot, Goldenrowley, Lenticel, J.delanoy, Steelwater~enwiki, Skier Dude, Touch Of Light, MezZzeR, Misspenny, Nortaak, Astroguyaz, ABF, TJ Elliot Scott, Bporopat, Goustien, Fratrep, Bill Sapperton, BHenry1969, ClueBot, Aljeirou, Banmeifucan, SchreiberBike, Knanshon, Badgernet, Lightbot, AnakngAraw, Citation bot, Drilnoth, Grim23, J04n, Pmlineditor, Spongefrog, Citation bot 1, Tbhotch, Zollerriia, ClueBot NG, Pulsecode, Helpful Pixie Bot, Fylbecatulous, RBKreckel and Anonymous: 44

- **Philippine mythical creatures** *Source:* https://en.wikipedia.org/wiki/Philippine_mythical_creatures?oldid=687257776 *Contributors:* Ahoerstemeier, Topbanana, Jondel, Woohookitty, BD2412, Rjwilmsi, RussBot, Nikkimaria, SmackBot, Hmains, OrphanBot, Rodsan18, Udibi, CmdrObot, Cydebot, Icqgirl, Nick Number, Goldenrowley, Alternativity, Fabrictramp, Lenticel, Joemaza, Kguirnela, Skier Dude, X!, VolkovBot, Philip Trueman, Giopotes, Aymatth2, AlexNewArtBot, Nedrutland, Mr.Kennedy1, Dr CareBear, ImageRemovalBot, The Thing That Should Not Be, Blanchardb, Axxand, Sun Creator, Johnuniq, XLinkBot, Addbot, Fyrael, Fraggle81, AnakngAraw, AnomieBOT, Eneasmarquez~enwiki, Gorrión, Tangent747, Blackguard SF, JL 09, Wireless Keyboard, I dream of horses, Elockid, Pikiwyn, Lotje, Diannaa, TheMesquito, DASH-Bot, Esoglou, Anirudh Emani, Cmlacy, Tolly4bolly, Z4ngetsu, Channik, Dawsondelph, Rhettsus1m, ClueBot NG, Helpful Pixie Bot, Carlojohnlapuerto, Paul-h0cdl, Pratyya Ghosh, Giovannicarlo888, Seguro64, Dexbot, LeFapOnymous, Samatict, SJ Defender, Renz Marion23, Hdidkbdhdir, Herseniada, Crisdador and Anonymous: 124

- **Philippine mythology** *Source:* https://en.wikipedia.org/wiki/Philippine_mythology?oldid=687718102 *Contributors:* DopefishJustin, Tregoweth, Ahoerstemeier, Big iron, Bloodshedder, RedWolf, Jondel, Gtrmp, Everyking, Jackol, Bluemask, Mike Rosoft, Gronky, Stereotek, SamEV, MBisanz, Matthewprc, NetBot, Jojit fb, Kundor, Eritain, Gary, Gunslinger47, Malo, Wtmitchell, Firsfron, Pufferfish101, Sjakkalle, Vary, Dar-Ape, Ian Pitchford, CalJW, RexNL, Mercury McKinnon, Pigman, Gaius Cornelius, Jaxl, Thiseye, EntChickie, Elektrocrow, Syrthiss, Capt crunch, Nlu, Ali K, E Wing, User24, SmackBot, Yamaguchi⬚⬚, Gilliam, Abaharaki, Ccscabang, J.smith, Will Beback, Ergative rlt, Rodsan18, Coyoty, Dboba, George The Dragon, Bendzh, Hmvillarante, Anak 1, Tawkerbot2, Lbr123, CRGreathouse, CmdrObot, Sir Vicious, Cydebot, Christian75, Tribu~enwiki, IndepIntel, 23prootie, Following specific instructions whispered by a mysterious cat, Baybayen, Infinitefate, Goldenrowley, Alphachimpbot, Maya alapaap, Mikomouse, VoABot II, Cloudhand, Alternativity, Zerocity, Johnbrillantes, Lenticel, Kguirnela, Bogey97, Largoplazo, Osay Magturo, Jjabellar, Idioma-bot, Jeff G., Aymatth2, Getonyourfeet, Witchy2006, Chris21jst, Jolog, Narutohaku, Phox46, Miniapolis, Dr CareBear, Maelgwnbot, Nefariousski, Denisarona, Sisigman, ClueBot, Wutsje, SoxBot, Kampfgruppe,

Egmontaz, 101boys, Little Mountain 5, Addbot, Nejibana17, Yobot, 2D, AnakngAraw, AnomieBOT, Vinniemon, Materialscientist, Eumolpo, Shoowak, LilHelpa, Niji18, The Evil IP address, Omnipaedista, FrescoBot, Pinethicket, Elockid, HRoestBot, JohnMarcelo, Fishspkr, Reach Out to the Truth, DARTH SIDIOUS 2, Ravishas3, Offtheheezy123xD, Listmeister, Talakaru, ClueBot NG, Janjanr, Dream of Nyx, Widr, Rurik the Varangian, Chitt66, HMSSolent, Jonarge, Greferjun, Mitchitara, Str62, GoShow, Frogger48, Lambrusia, Csw1854, MB298 and Anonymous: 224

- **Pugot** *Source:* https://en.wikipedia.org/wiki/Pugot?oldid=684244315 *Contributors:* The Anome, Kundor, LrdChaos, Asarelah, Deville, Smack-Bot, Bluebot, The Rogue Penguin, Rodsan18, CmdrObot, Cydebot, Goldenrowley, VoABot II, The Anomebot2, Lenticel, ImageRemovalBot, Addbot, II MusLiM HyBRiD II, ZéroBot, Monkbot and Anonymous: 10

- **Santelmo** *Source:* https://en.wikipedia.org/wiki/Santelmo?oldid=660421653 *Contributors:* Rmhermen, Alexf, Famousdog, Andrewpmk, Woohookitty, Rjwilmsi, TexasAndroid, Hmains, Chris the speller, Kilonum, Cydebot, Gavia immer, Magasin, CommonsDelinker, Slow Riot, ImageRemoval-Bot, Place Clichy, Excirial, Againme, AnomieBOT, Vinniemorano, Vinniemon, SporkBot, ClueBot NG, Allenjambalaya, MrBill3, Maxraydan and Anonymous: 12

- **Sarangay** *Source:* https://en.wikipedia.org/wiki/Sarangay?oldid=545447597 *Contributors:* Reinyday, JamesBurns, RussBot, Cydebot, Kguir-nela, ImageRemovalBot, Axxand, Addbot, Yobot, Vinniemon, ZéroBot and Anonymous: 2

- **Sarimanok** *Source:* https://en.wikipedia.org/wiki/Sarimanok?oldid=677131976 *Contributors:* Pratyeka, Jonathunder, George Hernandez, Mpatel, NickelShoe, SmackBot, Dun harold, The Rogue Penguin, OrphanBot, Nixeagle, WayKurat, Swatjester, Ser Amantio di Nicolao, Rodsan18, Joseph Solis in Australia, LadyofShalott, JForget, CmdrObot, Namayan, Cydebot, PamD, Coelacan, Richard Relucio, Golden-rowley, JamesBWatson, Lenticel, Rettetast, Aminullah, Vdhillon, Laoris, JD554, Unauthored, ClueBot, Addbot, Cst17, THEN WHO WAS PHONE?, AnomieBOT, Hariboneagle927, MikeyMouse10, Susumebashi, AnnaJune, ClueBot NG, Metricopolus, ChrisGualtieri, RioHondo, Grassboy1234, Tentinator, Trivolution and Anonymous: 41

- **Sigbin** *Source:* https://en.wikipedia.org/wiki/Sigbin?oldid=683277488 *Contributors:* Heron, Kundor, BD2412, Bhadani, TexasAndroid, Smack-Bot, Titopao, The Rogue Penguin, J. Spencer, Rodsan18, DangerousPanda, Cydebot, 23prootie, Mojo Hand, Alternativity, Lenticel, Commons-Delinker, Kguirnela, KylieTastic, Moonriddengirl, ImageRemovalBot, Cantseetheforest, Axxand, Arjayay, Addbot, FluffyWhiteCat, Tassede-the, Jackelfive, Vinniemorano, Vinniemon, FrescoBot, RedBot, Full-date unlinking bot, DARTH SIDIOUS 2, ClueBot NG, Bonvallite, King-domofsamoa, WikiUserThinking, Konveyor Belt, Ciaraleone, Stoppableforce, Vanhenry14 and Anonymous: 36

- **Sirena (Philippine mythology)** *Source:* https://en.wikipedia.org/wiki/Sirena_(Philippine_mythology)?oldid=685819642 *Contributors:* BD2412, RussBot, Asarelah, Cydebot, CommonsDelinker, Rtoledosj, Auntof6, Axxand, Addbot, AnakngAraw, AnomieBOT, Vinniemon, Shang-hainese.ua, Gwen-chan, ClueBot NG, Kjojo and Anonymous: 12

- **Siyokoy (Philippine mythology)** *Source:* https://en.wikipedia.org/wiki/Siyokoy_(Philippine_mythology)?oldid=606068994 *Contributors:* BD2412, Rjwilmsi, GiantSnowman, Cydebot, ImageRemovalBot, Axxand, Addbot, Luckas-bot, Vinniemon, PigFlu Oink and Anonymous: 6

- **Tagbanwa mythology** *Source:* https://en.wikipedia.org/wiki/Tagbanwa_mythology?oldid=505664993 *Contributors:* Bazonka, Cydebot, Richard Relucio, Mario1952, Mild Bill Hiccup, NuclearWarfare, ChrisGualtieri and Anonymous: 2

- **Tikbalang** *Source:* https://en.wikipedia.org/wiki/Tikbalang?oldid=687327013 *Contributors:* Jondel, DocWatson42, PFHLai, Bluemask, Kun-dor, Drat, Blaxthos, Woohookitty, BillC, Rjwilmsi, Echo5ive, NawlinWiki, Sleepwalkingdreamer, Tony1, SmackBot, The Rogue Penguin, Fronkey, WayKurat, Rodsan18, Nehrams2020, Joseph Solis in Australia, Cydebot, Beached Oil Tanker, VZG, Kotengu, Goldenrowley, Robina Fox, Alternativity, Johnbrillantes, Lenticel, R'n'B, Kguirnela, Steelwater~enwiki, Berserkerz Crit, Idioma-bot, Jeff G., Joshua manimtim2, Phox46, Calliopejen1, Moonriddengirl, ClueBot, MikeVitale, Axxand, Sebleouf, XLinkBot, Addbot, Ettrig, Contributor777, AnakngAraw, AnomieBOT, Jim1138, Mintrick, Citation bot, Niji18, FrescoBot, Wireless Keyboard, Citation bot 1, Jonesey95, Diannaa, John of Read-ing, Werieth, ZéroBot, ClueBot NG, Helpful Pixie Bot, BG19bot, Mysterytrey, Megamanxs, Cyberbot II, Dexbot, Mogism, Cerbera LM, WikiUserThinking, VarthDaver, Hoho24, My name is not dave, KimSMtH, Ryan Ch'ng and Anonymous: 80

- **Tiyanak** *Source:* https://en.wikipedia.org/wiki/Tiyanak?oldid=676560879 *Contributors:* MisfitToys, BD2412, RussBot, Moe Epsilon, Smack-Bot, The Rogue Penguin, WayKurat, Rodsan18, Cydebot, Biruitorul, Woody, Sigurd Dragon Slayer, Alternativity, Lenticel, CommonsDelinker, ImageRemovalBot, Ettrig, AnakngAraw, IronLotus, AnomieBOT, Vinniemorano, Citation bot, Yo 17, J04n, FrescoBot, Citation bot 1, Ob-sidian Soul, EmausBot, Orange Suede Sofa, Mtking, Marveilleux, CitationCleanerBot, Ajbilan, Monkbot and Anonymous: 21

- **Wakwak** *Source:* https://en.wikipedia.org/wiki/Wakwak?oldid=670430917 *Contributors:* William Avery, Frecklefoot, Friday, Yamaguchi⬚⬚, Cydebot, Racepacket, Editor437, Dr CareBear, Middayexpress, Marden16, FrescoBot, Card Zero, ClueBot NG and Anonymous: 5

39.4.2 Images

- **File:0045MuseumFilipinojf_08.JPG** *Source:* https://upload.wikimedia.org/wikipedia/commons/3/35/0045MuseumFilipinojf_08.JPG *License:* CC BY-SA 3.0 *Contributors:* Own work *Original artist:* Ramon FVelasquez

- **File:Ambox_important.svg** *Source:* https://upload.wikimedia.org/wikipedia/commons/b/b4/Ambox_important.svg *License:* Public domain *Contributors:* Own work, based off of Image:Ambox scales.svg *Original artist:* Dsmurat (talk · contribs)

- **File:Autoroute_icone.svg** *Source:* https://upload.wikimedia.org/wikipedia/commons/7/7f/Autoroute_icone.svg *License:* CC BY-SA 2.5 *Con-tributors:* SVG version of File:Road stub mini pictogram.png *Original artist:* Dake (talk · contribs), Booyabazooka (talk · contribs), Roulex 45 (talk · contribs), and Doodledoo (talk · contribs)

- **File:Balete_drive.png** *Source:* https://upload.wikimedia.org/wikipedia/en/3/30/Balete_drive.png *License:* CC-BY-SA-3.0 *Contributors:* While strolling
  Previously published: none
  Original artist:
  Kj plma

39.4.3 Content license

www.ingramcontent.com/pod-product-compliance
Lightning Source LLC
Chambersburg PA
CBHW081226280526
45787CB00006B/2545